RAND

Domestic Terrorism

A National Assessment of State and Local Preparedness

Kevin Jack Riley, Bruce Hoffman

Supported by the
National Institute of Justice,
U.S. Department of Justice

The research described in this report was supported by the National Institute of Justice, U.S. Department of Justice, under Grant 84-IJ-CX-0072.

Library of Congress Cataloging in Publication Data

Riley, Kevin Jack, 1964–
    Domestic terrorism : a national assessment of state and local
preparedness / Kevin Jack Riley, Bruce R. Hoffman.
        p.   cm
    MR-505-NIJ.
    "Sponsored by the National Institute of Justice"—CIP t.p.
    ISBN 0-8330-1627-X
    1. Terrorism—United States.   2. Terrorism—Prevention—
United States.   I. Hoffman, Bruce, 1954–   .   II. National
Institute of Justice (U.S.)   III. Title.
HV6432.R55   1995
363.3´2´0973—dc20   94-47133
                                                                                        CIP

RAND
Copyright © 1995

RAND is a nonprofit institution that helps improve public policy through research and analysis. RAND's publications do not necessarily reflect the opinions or policies of its research sponsors.

Published 1995 by RAND
1700 Main Street, P.O. Box 2138, Santa Monica, CA 90407-2138
RAND URL: http://www.rand.org/
To order RAND documents or to obtain additional information, contact Distribution
Services: Telephone: (310) 451-7002; Fax: (310) 451-6915; Internet: order@rand.org/

Preface

The research described in this report was supported by a grant from the National Institute of Justice under a project entitled "Domestic Terrorism: A National Assessment of State and Local Law Enforcement Preparedness" that was conducted in RAND's Criminal Justice Research Program. The purpose of this project was to analyze states' and municipalities' terrorism preparedness as a means of providing law enforcement with information about the prevention and control of terrorist activities in the United States. The research involved a three-phased approach, including a national survey of state and local law enforcement agencies to arrive at a net assessment of the terrorist threat in this country as perceived by these jurisdictions; exploration, identification, and description, through case studies, of notable instances of liaison, guideline development and implementation, training, and cooperation between state, local, and federal authorities with respect to anti- and counter-terrorism programs; the identification and description of promising anti-terrorist and counter-terrorist programs through case studies of local jurisdictions; and the identification of programs to counter potential future threats as well as the development of a future research agenda.

Contents

Tables

Summary

Recent events such as the bombing of the World Trade Center and the arrest of Los Angeles members of the Fourth Reich compellingly demonstrate that the threat of terrorism in the United States is not negligible. These events and others have led to heightened security measures in the United States. The concern generated by terrorism has focused attention on federal, state, and local law enforcement preventive and preparedness measures and, in particular, on the reevaluation of domestic security policies and procedures nationwide. The FBI and many large police departments, through joint terrorism task forces, have taken significant steps to develop plans and countermeasures to protect the most vulnerable or likely terrorist targets. However, equally attractive and lucrative potential targets—such as military installations, fuel supplies, telecommunications nodes, power plants, and other vital infrastructure—exist in smaller less-populated jurisdictions.

This document reports the results of a 24-month research effort to survey and analyze the key problems and issues confronting state and local law enforcement agencies in countering the threat of terrorism in the United States. The project specifically sought to analyze states' and municipalities' terrorism preparedness as a means of providing law enforcement with information about the prevention and control of terrorist activities in the United States. This was accomplished through the project's three principal research tasks:

- A national survey of state and local law enforcement agencies designed to assess how law enforcement agencies below the federal level perceive the threat of terrorism in the United States and to identify potentially promising anti- and counter-terrorism programs currently used by these jurisdictions;

- The selection of ten locations, chosen after the survey, as case studies to examine in detail how different jurisdictions have adapted to the threat of terrorism and to elucidate further the anti- and counter-terrorism programs used by these select jurisdictions;

- The identification of programs used by state and local law enforcement agencies to counter potential future threats, along with the development of a prospective future research agenda.

The survey results indicate that a sizable majority of state and municipal law enforcement organizations consider terrorism, or the threat thereof, to be a problem. Of particular note is that many state and local law enforcement organizations consider a wider range of activities and acts as terrorist, or potentially terrorist, than does the FBI. Thus, although official FBI terrorist statistics point to low levels of terrorist activity, attribute many recent acts of terrorism to Puerto Rican nationalists, and do not count many threatening acts by organizations such as the Skinheads as terrorist, states and municipalities are equally adamant in identifying right-wing (Neo-Nazi, anti-Semitic, anti-federalist) and issue-specific (anti-abortion, animal rights, environmentalist) organizations as the most threatening actual and potential terrorist sources.

While in agreement that terrorism presents a challenge to law enforcement organizations, the states and municipalities diverge in their approaches to the problems. The findings demonstrate that smaller jurisdictions, which may house sensitive facilities such as nuclear power plants, communications nodes, and other potential targets, have different approaches to terrorism preparedness than do large cities. These differences are evident in areas ranging from development of guidelines and contingency plans to training and operations.

The case studies confirm in detail what the survey revealed in general terms. That is, communities perceive potential terrorism problems and have an interest in confronting terrorism before it erupts, but in many cases are forced by budgetary, manpower, and other constraints to limit their terrorism preparedness. In such instances, cooperation with the FBI, through regular communication, training, and guidelines, is highly valued. Despite the resource and other constraints noted, the case studies reveal that a variety of successful terrorism preparedness formulas exist in communities both large and small. Large municipalities, such as New York City and Miami, have developed significant terrorism programs in close cooperation with the FBI and its regional joint terrorism task forces, whereas smaller communities, such as Kootenai County/Coeur d'Alene, Idaho, have worked to stay ahead of nascent terrorism threats by forging close regional alliances and capitalizing on available FBI resources.

More generally, the case study findings suggest that a community's size, its resources, and the nature of the terrorism threats it confronts will influence both the strategic and tactical law enforcement response. Communities value the intelligence and support that the FBI provides, and municipalities highly value their communication with federal authorities. Localities are interested in adopting a strategic approach, in which intelligence, planning, and advance preparation are used to combat terrorism, but lack the resources in many cases to maintain this more expensive approach.

Acknowledgments

Many thanks are due the anonymous respondents to our survey about terrorism and terrorism preparedness. Without their participation, this project would not have been possible. Dan McCaffrey and Doug Longshore provided thoughtful and comprehensive reviews that aided the authors immeasurably. In addition, Karen Gardela deserves special mention for her efforts in extracting supplementary data from the RAND terrorism database. Finally, thanks are due Patricia Bedrosian for the outstanding editing she provided. While those mentioned contributed materially to the improvement of this work, the authors alone are solely responsible for errors in interpretation and exposition.

1. Introduction

This document reports the results of a 24-month research effort to survey and analyze the key problems and issues confronting state and local law enforcement agencies in countering the threat of terrorism in the United States.[1] The project specifically sought to identify and describe how different jurisdictions have adapted to the threat of terrorism and which anti- and counter-terrorism programs have been employed by these jurisdictions. This was accomplished through the project's three principal research tasks:

- A national survey of state and local law enforcement agencies designed to assess how law enforcement agencies below the federal level perceive the threat of terrorism in the United States and to identify potentially promising anti- and counter-terrorism programs currently used by these jurisdictions;

- The selection of ten locations, chosen after the survey, as case studies to examine in detail how different jurisdictions have adapted to the threat of terrorism and to elucidate further the anti- and counter-terrorism programs used by these select jurisdictions;

- The identification of programs used by state and local law enforcement agencies to counter potential future threats along with the development of a prospective future research agenda.

This report is divided into five sections. Section 2 describes the methodology of the study, including the survey design, data gathering, and sampling procedures. Section 3 analyzes the results of the national survey pertaining to state and local perceptions of the terrorist threat in the United States, conducted as part of this project. Section 4 summarizes state and local law enforcement preparedness for countering and responding to terrorism. Section 4 also uses the case studies to identify noteworthy strengths and weaknesses in counter- and anti-terrorism preparedness in areas such as contingency planning, planning review, guideline development, terrorism unit formation and operation, and training. The final section assesses the policy implications of this research and proposes a prospective future research agenda based on these conclusions.

---

[1]Research for this project was completed in January 1993, one month before the bombing of the World Trade Center in New York City. The results therefore do not reflect the effect that this incident may have had on state and local law enforcement terrorism planning or response measures.

2. Survey Methodology, Data Gathering, and Sampling

The first phase of this project involved the design of a national survey of state and local law enforcement and emergency management agencies. The purpose of the survey was twofold: first, to discover how agencies at these two levels of government perceive the terrorist threat in the United States; and second, to learn how these agencies both manage the threat of terrorism and plan and organize their response to actual incidents. This was a means of identifying potentially noteworthy instances of jurisdictions adapting to the threat of terrorism and employing anti- and counter-terrorism programs that would be investigated further through a series of case studies. Throughout the survey design process, advice and direction from both the U.S. Federal Bureau of Investigation (FBI), and the U.S. Department of Justice, National Institute of Justice (NIJ), was solicited and received. The final survey instrument was reviewed at least twice by the FBI, the NIJ, and the project's advisory panel of experts in the field of law enforcement and terrorism. A critical issue that emerged at the outset of the survey design was in defining terrorism.

Defining Terrorism

Few words in recent years have been as promiscuously used or have assumed as pejorative a connotation as "terrorism." Nearly two decades ago, terrorism expert Brian Jenkins lamented that terrorism had become a "fad" word, indiscriminately applied to a range of acts and motivations often beyond the political character essential in distinguishing terrorism from other acts of criminal, but non-politically motivated, violence. The problem is that there exists no precise or widely accepted definition of terrorism. Some governments, for example, label as terrorism all violence committed by their political opponents, whereas antigovernment extremists frequently claim to be the victims of government terror. What is called terrorism thus often seems to depend on one's point of view.

Hence, common usage of the word terrorism is more a catchall than a precise definition, referring to a variety of violent acts perpetrated by states, their political opponents, and ostensibly non-political criminals as well. It is this political element that distinguishes economically motivated crimes from politically motivated (i.e., terrorist) violence. The ordinary criminal certainly uses short-term terror to achieve his goals, be it brandishing a knife in front of a mugging victim or using a gun in a bank robbery. But the purpose of the criminal act does not go beyond the act itself or the acquisition of money and other valuables. The terrorist act is different in that the violence employed is not only in pursuit of some long-range *political* goal but is designed to have far-reaching psychological repercussions on a particular target audience.

In sum, terrorism is violence, or the threat of violence, calculated to create an atmosphere of fear and alarm. These acts are designed to coerce others into taking actions they would otherwise not undertake or to refrain from taking actions that they desire to take. All terrorist acts are crimes. Many would also be violations of the rules of war, if a state of war existed. This violence or threat of violence is generally directed against civilian targets. The motives of all terrorists are political, and terrorist actions are generally carried out in a way that will achieve maximum publicity. The perpetrators are members of an organized group, and, unlike other criminals, they often claim credit for their acts. Finally, terrorist acts are intended to produce effects beyond the immediate physical damage they cause by having long-term psychological repercussions on a particular target audience. The fear created by terrorists, for example, may be intended to cause people to exaggerate the strength of the terrorists and the importance of their cause, to provoke governmental overreaction, to discourage dissent, or simply to intimidate and thereby enforce compliance with their demands.

Amid the array of definitions that have been applied to terrorism and the issues of individual perception and prejudice that inevitably influence such definitions, the FBI has developed its own legal definition of terrorism. This definition not only reflects U.S. Congressional legislation but that of senior-level government advisory and consulting bodies such as the Vice President's Task Force on Terrorism. In the survey, the definition of terrorism we used was that used by the FBI: "Terrorism is the unlawful use of force or violence against persons or property to intimidate or coerce a government, the civilian population, or any segment thereof in furtherance of political or social objectives."[1]

The official FBI definition of terrorism excludes many hateful acts and crimes that might, at first glance, appear to meet the bureau's definition. For instance,

---

[1]Terrorist Research and Analytical Center, Counter-Terrorism Section Intelligence Division, *Terrorism in the United States 1982–1992* (Washington, D.C.: U.S. Department of Justice, Federal Bureau of Investigation, 1993), Appendix A, p. 20. Additionally, the FBI distinguishes two types of terrorism. Domestic terrorism is defined as involving groups or individuals whose terrorist activities are directed at elements of our government or population without foreign direction. International terrorism is defined as involving terrorist activities committed by groups or individuals who are foreign based and/or directed by countries or groups outside the United States or whose activities transcend national boundaries.

racially or religiously motivated acts of violence, so-called hate crimes perpetrated by Skinheads and white supremacist gangs, appear to be violent acts intended to further political objectives at the citizens' expense. Similarly, other acts of apparent politically motivated violence, such as attacks on medical clinics performing abortions, attacks on laboratories and clinics performing experiments on animals, and the sabotaging of logging operations, might also appear to meet the definition. Exactly why such crimes do not count, in some instances, as terrorism is a matter of some dispute. Generally, in addition to the definition cited above, the FBI also seeks a conspiratorial dimension when evaluating potential acts of terrorism. The conspiratorial dimension might include evidence that more than one crime was intended to be committed, or evidence that a network of individuals prepared to carry out additional acts stands behind lone perpetrators. Thus, the murder of abortionist Dr. Gunn in Pensacola, Florida, was considered an isolated criminal act, in large part because evidence depicting a conspiracy was lacking.

The definitional matter is further complicated by the fact that no such crime as terrorism actually exists according to U.S. statutes. Terrorists are not convicted of "terrorism" but rather are convicted of the accompanying crimes, such as murder, weapons violations, and so forth, that constitute their terrorist acts. In recent years, certain criminal acts have begun to meet the official definition as evidence of a conspiratorial element has grown. For example, the 1993 report *Terrorism in the United States* includes incidents by the Animal Liberation Front and the American Front Skinheads. In contrast, much of the terrorism reported in the 1980s was committed by ethnic/emigre groups.

The FBI investigates far more criminal acts as potential terrorist incidents than it actually classifies as such. Many incidents are reported to the FBI, which, upon further investigation, and in accordance with the aforementioned guidelines laid down for defining a criminal act as a terrorist incident, are reclassified as ordinary crimes. Incidents such as these, which are reported to the FBI as potential terrorist incidents, should not be overlooked. Among other factors, such reports can provide important early warnings to the FBI that an organized terrorism effort is emerging. Moreover, these reports are also important indications of what state and local officials *perceive* as acts of terrorism. To incorporate jurisdictions' perceptions of terrorism that are reflected in the reporting of suspected incidents, this document will use a definition of terrorism that is slightly broader than the official one. That is, in the context of this document, "terrorism" should be imbued not only with the official FBI definition but with the more expansive meaning imparted by suspected incidents and municipalities' perceptions.

A similar definitional exercise must be undertaken for law enforcement efforts to control terrorism. *Anti-terrorism* measures are generally taken to mean activities that seek to *prevent* the execution of terrorist acts. *Counter-terrorism* measures are activities that *respond* to terrorist acts once they have occurred. The distinction becomes particularly relevant in the latter sections of this report when planning, training, and operational issues relating to terrorism preparedness are discussed.

Sample Units

Three distinct jurisdictions with overlapping responsibilities for terrorism preparedness were sampled for this analysis. Two of the jurisdictions are at the state level and one is at the local level. State law enforcement agencies constitute the first jurisdiction sampled. Organizations included in this group are primarily concerned with enforcing laws and maintaining public order. In most cases the organization surveyed was the State Police. Throughout the analysis, this group of sample respondents is referred to as "state law enforcement agencies." The second sampling unit considers those organizations with emergency preparedness responsibilities. Organizations from this group have statewide authority but limited powers of law enforcement. Examples include state Departments of Public Safety, Departments of Justice, and state emergency management organizations. They were included in this study because they prepare and train for many emergencies that are similar or analogous to the potential repercussions of major terrorist incidents. These organizations are referred to as "state emergency management organizations." Local law enforcement agencies constitute the last sampling group. Local law enforcement agencies have law enforcement authority which may extend to city, county, or township boundaries, but which does not extend to statewide matters. Municipal police and sheriff departments are examples from this group. These respondents are variously referred to as "local" and "municipal law enforcement agencies."

Selection of State Law Enforcement and Emergency Management Agencies

At the state level, 52 law enforcement agencies were identified. These 52 agencies constitute the universe of state law enforcement agencies rather than a sample. That is, each state, the District of Columbia, and Puerto Rico has one statewide law enforcement authority and each was surveyed in this process. The same is true for the state emergency management offices: 52 offices were identified and surveyed covering the 50 states, Washington, D.C., and Puerto

Rico. Thus, no special sampling techniques were needed to survey state-level organizations.

Selection of Local Jurisdictions

It was impossible to survey the universe of local law enforcement agencies because there are literally thousands of such organizations. At the same time, simple random sampling of all municipal and county law enforcement organizations was not appropriate. Terrorist threats are relatively rare and the pool of municipal law enforcement agencies so large that an extremely large sample would have been necessary to elicit even small amounts of information about terrorism instances and terrorism preparedness. To get better information on terrorist threats and preparedness against such threats, it was necessary to oversample from the population of municipalities coping with these issues. Thus, the pool of potential respondents was narrowed through the use of a two-part sampling frame. In part one of the sampling frame, local jurisdictions were organized according to population and jurisdictions were selected from the population pools on the basis of criteria outlined below. This sample is referred to as population-based. In part two of the sampling frame, a list of specific jurisdictions deemed to be more susceptible to terrorist threats was established and each of these municipalities was surveyed. This is the targeted sample. In total, 299 local jurisdictions were contacted and asked to respond to the survey. Of these, 160 were from the population pool and 139 were from the targeted pool.

By deliberately sampling among populations that were more likely to be targets of terrorism, we are introducing a bias. That is, we will find more terrorism than actually exists because we deliberately sought out jurisdictions where the threat was higher. In cases where the bias is relevant, and where an unbiased response will be of interest, the findings will separately report the population-based and targeted groups' responses.

Sampling from the Population Pool

Using census divisions, the country was divided into four regions: Midwest, Northeast, South, and West.[2] Twelve counties were selected from each census

---

[2]Midwest: Illinois, Indiana, Iowa, Kansas, Michigan, Minnesota, Missouri, Nebraska, North Dakota, Ohio, South Dakota, and Wisconsin. Northeast: Connecticut, Maine, Massachusetts, New Hampshire, New Jersey, New York, Pennsylvania, Rhode Island and Vermont. South: Alabama, Arkansas, Delaware, District of Columbia, Florida, Georgia, Kentucky, Louisiana, Maryland, Mississippi, North Carolina, Oklahoma, Puerto Rico, South Carolina, Tennessee, Texas, Virginia, and West Virginia. West: Alaska, Arizona, California, Colorado, Idaho, Hawaii, Montana, Nevada, New Mexico, Oregon, Utah, Washington, and Wyoming.

division, for a total of 48 counties in the population sampling pool. The 12 counties from each region were selected in four steps. First, the three largest counties from each region were selected, subject to the constraint that no two came from the same state. Using population estimates from the 1990 census, this procedure resulted in the selections reported in Table 2.1.

Next, in each region the set of remaining counties in which the population exceeded 500,000 was identified. From each regional pool, a simple random sample of three counties was drawn. The procedure was repeated for counties whose populations lie between 100,000 and 500,000 and for counties with a population less than 100,000. The final sample thus contains the 12 largest counties, 12 counties with populations greater than 500,000, 12 with populations between 100,000 and 500,000, and 12 with populations under 100,000. Using this sampling frame, every county in the nation had a non-zero probability of landing in our sample.

The final step was to identify the law enforcement agencies from each of the 48 counties that would be asked to respond to the survey. For each county, the municipal or county enforcement agency of the county seat and two additional jurisdictions were selected and asked to complete the survey. The selection process of these jurisdictions was, when possible, random. In some cases, most notably in the largest and the smallest counties, there were few jurisdictions eligible for inclusion. Very small towns typically do not have municipal police forces and instead rely on county or state law enforcement organizations for police services. Similarly, some of the largest counties, such as Philadelphia, had very few law enforcement organizations because the county is served by one or two large units.

Once the list of jurisdictions was complete, the appropriate Chiefs of Police, Sheriffs, or division heads to be surveyed were identified from *The National Directory of Law Enforcement Administrators and Correctional Agencies*. This reference is published yearly by the National Police Chiefs and Sheriffs

Table 2.1

Largest Counties Selected for Sampling

Northeast	Midwest	South	West
Middlesex, MA	Wayne, MI	Dade, FL	Los Angeles, CA
Kings, NY	Cook, IL	Harris, TX	Maricopa, AZ
Philadelphia, PA	Cuyahoga, OH	Shelby, TN	King, WA

Information Bureau. These officials were sent the surveys and asked to complete them.

Selection of the Targeted Organizations

To supplement our population-based sample, we targeted 139 locations that have experienced terrorist activity in the past, or that house potential terrorist targets. These locations include counties and towns where terrorist groups are known to be located, as well as counties with nuclear facilities, military installations, or other institutions that make logical terrorist targets. These jurisdictions were identified through both annual FBI reports of terrorism in the United States[3] and use of the RAND terrorism database, which contains records of terrorism incidents in the United States. Within each targeted jurisdiction, the survey respondents were again identified from *The National Directory of Law Enforcement Administrators and Correctional Agencies.*

Survey Procedures

The survey process consisted of three mailings. Each site received an initial packet that included the survey instrument, a letter requesting their participation, a statement of confidentiality, and a brief description of RAND. Ten days after the first packet was sent, a second letter was sent. This letter served as a reminder to those who had not yet responded and a thank you to those who had. Three weeks from the initial mailing, a second packet containing the same materials as the first was mailed to all who had not responded to the initial survey. Two weeks after the second packet was sent, follow-up phone calls were made to the remaining agencies that had not responded. If an agency failed to respond 20 days after the follow-up phone call, it was replaced with a jurisdiction previously selected in the sampling process.

Response Rates

At the state level, of the 52 law enforcement agencies surveyed, 39, or 75 percent, responded with completed or partially completed surveys. Of the 13 state

---

[3]Federal Bureau of Investigation, Terrorist Research and Analytical Center, Counter-Terrorism Section, Criminal Investigation Division, *Terrorism in the United States* (Washington, D.C.: U.S. Department of Justice, Federal Bureau of Investigation, 1993), reports for the years 1980–1989, inclusive.

agencies that did not complete the survey, five returned incomplete or blank instruments, five responded by stating that they would decline to answer the survey, and three did not return the survey.

The response rate of the state emergency management offices was similar to that of the state law enforcement agencies. Of the 52 agencies, 37 (71 percent) responded with completed questionnaires. The nonrespondents from this group included six that returned incomplete or blank instruments, six that responded by stating that they would decline to answer the survey, and one that simply did not return the survey.

The response rates for the local law enforcement agencies was lower than the rate of the state agencies. Eighty-four municipalities from the population-based pool responded, from a total of 160 queried, resulting in a 53 percent response rate. Sixty-four agencies from the targeted group responded, from 139 sampled, resulting in a 46 percent response rate. Table 2.2 summarizes the response rate.

A number of factors explain the lower response rates at the municipal and county levels. In many cases the agency respondents erroneously assumed that because they had no terrorist groups and no special training, their participation was not desired. Others noted that theirs was not the appropriate agency. For example, in Pennsylvania, county law enforcement organizations have no investigative responsibilities. Similarly, other county agencies wrote that they had a role only in corrections. The lower response rate might also be attributed to the large number of surveys these agencies receive each year. One police department respondent noted that this was seventh survey received by his department during 1992. Several police departments specifically stated that they were currently working on a very large survey sent out by the Los Angeles Police Department. One respondent complained about the time and manpower needed to complete that questionnaire and thought they should be compensated for the

Table 2.2

Survey Response Rates

Agency	Surveyed	Responded	Rate (%)
State law enforcement	52	39	75
State emergency management	52	37	71
Local law enforcement (population-based)	160	84	53
Local law enforcement (targeted)	139	64	46

time spent. In another case, the local agency refused to comply because it believed that the information we were asking for was too sensitive to be released.

Refusals and Nonresponse

The purpose of sampling is to use respondents as representatives of a larger population because of the inability to survey large populations in their entirety. When the characteristics of the respondent group are very similar to the characteristics of the entire population, the sample provides a good, unbiased approximation of how the entire population would answer if it had been surveyed. But bias can be introduced into survey results if those who choose not to respond to the survey are somehow different from those who do respond. That is, if the characteristics of the nonrespondents are somehow different from the characteristics of the respondents, there is a potential for bias to be introduced.

Ideally, nonresponses will be in proportion to the group's share in the sampling population. To take an example, we would hope that sheriffs departments in small counties, which account for 20 percent of the sample population, would also account for approximately 20 percent of the nonresponse pool. If small counties accounted for, say, 70 percent of the nonrespondents, the ability to generalize about small counties and their terrorism perspectives might be jeopardized. Even if nonresponse rates are distributed in relatively correct proportions across the relevant demographic groups, the response and nonresponse pools may well differ along dimensions that are not apparent but that might have been elicited by the survey. Thus, the ability to evaluate the distortions caused by nonresponse is limited precisely because a portion of the population chooses not to participate. Among the population-based sample, the potential for nonresponse bias was mitigated by the replacement mechanism used. When a municipality refused to complete the survey, it was replaced with a similar municipality selected using the sampling frame. Obviously, no two municipalities will be the same, but selecting them from the same region of the country and from the same population category helps reduce the differences. No such mechanism was used to replace targeted respondents that refused to participate. Nevertheless, the targeted communities already shared the important characteristic that they were more likely to have experienced terrorism, or to house a facility that might be a potential terrorist target. Caution should be used when attempting to generalize or extrapolate these survey results both because inclusion of the targeted sample, as previously noted, was intended to oversample among communities more likely to experience terrorism, and because exclusion of the targeted sample leaves very small cell sizes for many of the survey questions.

Within the descriptive context, the survey was extremely valuable at eliciting information about terrorism and preparedness. Each respondent described the roles and responsibilities of agencies and departments involved in anti- and counter-terrorist planning and procedures, the education and training of personnel involved in anti- and counter-terrorist planning, the procedures and responses used in planning and policy, the methods of planning and control, perceptions of terrorist threats, risk assessment activities intended to identify threats and the criticality and vulnerability of possible targets, the factors considered in selecting risk-reduction strategies, and an evaluation of the performance, effectiveness, and cost of preventive measures. Combined, these results provide a compelling picture of terrorism preparedness at the state and local levels.

Selection of Case Studies

Using our analysis of the survey results and in consultation with the FBI and the project's advisory board, we selected 10 locations as case studies for more detailed examination. The primary objective for the cases studies was to study how different jurisdictions have adapted to the threat of terrorism. The considerations used to guide our case study selections were:

- Jurisdictions where terrorist groups are located and terrorist activity has been reported in the past;

- Identification from the survey of contingency plans, potential model programs, and guidelines developed to deal with terrorism;

- Training, both generalized and specialized, in anti- and counter-terrorism that personnel in the departments surveyed have received;

- Threat assessments that have been conducted by the departments surveyed; and

- Targets that have been identified by the departments and agencies surveyed as potentially attractive to terrorists or that are regarded as potentially vulnerable.

From the survey responses we developed a list of jurisdictions that provide us with the range of variables we identified in consultation with the FBI and NIJ as germane to terrorism preparedness. For example, we looked at jurisdictions with a high level of terrorist activity, regardless of whether special training is available or used by local agencies. We also looked at those jurisdictions where departments and agencies are particularly well-trained, have developed contingency plans and other guidelines, and maintain current threat assessments, but where only modest amounts of terrorist activity were reported. In addition, we selected locations that would provide wide geographical and population representation. Accordingly, we selected two to three sites in each major region of the United States (Northeast, South, Midwest, and West), with populations ranging in size from 8,400 to 7 million.

The following case study locations were selected. For reasons of security and concern over the publication of sensitive personnel size, organization, specific training received, and contingency plans developed, a number of details are necessarily omitted from the description that follows, and indeed, throughout the report. Wherever any of these sensitive issues of training and preparedness are discussed, the specific case study location is not identified. The 10 case studies included:

- Whitehall, Pennsylvania (population: 15,000)

- New York, New York (population: 7,323,000)

- Birmingham, Alabama (population: 266,000)

- Miami, Florida (population: 359,000)

- San Juan, Puerto Rico (population: 434,725)

- Milwaukee, Wisconsin (population: 636,236)

- Coffey County/Burlington, Kansas (population: 8,400)

- Coeur d'Alene, Idaho (population: 20,054)

- Seattle, Washington (population: 493,846)

- Los Angeles, California (population: 3,485,000)

Following the selection of the case study locations, we visited each of the sites. The purpose of these visits was to learn first-hand how each department and agency operates. A semi-structured site visit questionnaire was developed and each visit included interviews with program administrators, line staff, supervisors, and personnel. Where available, documentation was obtained detailing program and guidelines development, policy, organizational structure, operating procedures, threat assessment and vulnerable assets identification, and contingency planning and formulation of emergency management procedures.

3. Perceptions of Domestic Terrorism

Overview

Although the United States is the country most frequently targeted abroad by terrorists, it is somewhere near the bottom of the list in the number of terrorist attacks annually recorded within its own borders. For example, according to the FBI, 12 terrorist attacks occurred in the United States in 1993; only four in 1992; five in 1991; seven in 1990; four in 1989; nine in 1987; and 25 in 1986. Moreover, until the 1993 bombing of New York's World Trade Center, where six persons died, no one had been killed in a terrorist incident in the United States since 1986.[1] Nevertheless, the United States is not immune to terrorism from within its own borders. A variety of ethnic/emigre groups, purely indigenous terrorist organizations, and foreign terrorist groups are committed to the use of violence in pursuit of their political objectives. Indeed, the continuing violence perpetrated by Puerto Rican separatists, opponents of legalized abortion, and foreign elements, as dramatically demonstrated by the February 1993 bombing of New York City's World Trade Center, underscores the fact that the threat of terrorism in this country can by no means be discounted.

There are five potential types of terrorist organizations in the United States:

- Ethnic separatist and emigre groups;

- Left-wing radical organizations;

- Right-wing racist, anti-authority, survivalist-type groups;

- Foreign terrorist organizations;

- Issue-oriented groups (including anti-abortionists,[2] animal rights, and environmental extremist groups).

---

[1]Federal Bureau of Investigation, Terrorist Research and Analytical Center, Counter-Terrorism Section, Intelligence Division, *Terrorism in the United States 1982–1992* (Washington, D.C.: U.S. Department of Justice, Federal Bureau of Investigation, 1993). By comparison, for example, an average of approximately 1.5 million crimes per year were recorded in the United States during the same period along with an annual average of about 20,000 homicides. See U.S. Department of Justice, *Uniform Crime Reports, 1989–1993.*

[2]To date, the FBI has not defined incidents of anti-abortion violence as terrorism. However, many survey respondents counted the anti-abortion movement as a potential terrorist threat, and thus it is included here.

In the past, the ethnic/emigre groups have generally been the most persistent and violent of the five group types, although this pattern may soon be challenged by right-wing groups. Historically, however, ethnic separatist groups have inflicted the most casualties and perpetrated the greatest number of officially recorded terrorist incidents. Their causes and grievances often have little or nothing to do with domestic U.S. politics. Rather, the United States is simply the battleground where their quarrels are fought. These groups also spawn successor generations of younger terrorists. However, despite their potentially wide appeal within their own communities, these organizations' narrow focus limits their political constituency solely to other ethnic/emigre groups in scattered tightly knit communities around the country.

In contrast, left-wing groups and issue-oriented terrorists (such as those opposed to legalized abortion, radical environmentalists, and militant animal rights activists) have a potentially broader constituency. Indigenous left-wing groups and issue-oriented terrorists supporting both "liberal" (e.g., environmental) and "conservative" (e.g., abortion opposition) issues are generally less lethal than their ethnic/emigre counterparts. They engage primarily in symbolic bombings to call attention to themselves and their causes, but they seldom undertake actions that could cause widespread, indiscriminate casualties. Although some of the leftist groups have justified their existence and operations with vague references to Marxist-Leninist dicta, others have been quite specific in their reactions to contentious political issues, including opposition to U.S. military involvement in Central America during the early and mid-1980s and to the former South African government's apartheid policy.

Right-wing terrorists appear to embrace the respective traits of both the ethnic separatist and left-wing terrorists. They are extremely violent, have no reservations about killing, spawn successor generations, and are often oriented toward specific political issues. These organizations span the spectrum ranging from traditional hate groups to anti-government groups supportive of the U.S. government's overthrow. During the past decade several racist and reactionary groups have surfaced, including anti-federalists, anti-Semites, racists, survivalists, and extreme, apocalyptic, Christian militants. Although related to the Ku Klux Klan and older American Nazi groups, the new organizations, including Skinheads, not only champion the old dogmas of a racially pure, Christian United States with no Jews, African-Americans, Hispanics, Asians, Catholics, or atheists, they are also violently opposed to any form of government above the county level.

Foreign terrorist groups, primarily Middle Eastern or Islamic entities, have also been active in the United States. At least four state-sponsored incidents took place in this country allegedly at the behest of Libya or Iran during the early 1980s. In July 1980, Ali Tabatabai, who served as press attaché for the Shah of Iran before the 1979 revolution that brought the Ayatollah Khomeini to power, was murdered in Washington, D.C., by David Belfield (also known as Daoud Salhudin). Belfield is an American Muslim with known ties to the Islamic Guerrillas in America, a pro-Khomeini group. Belfield later fled the country and is believed to have gone to Iran. Less than two weeks later an attempt was made on the life of another Iranian opponent of Khomeini, Shah Reis, in Los Angeles. In October 1980, a Libyan graduate student and opponent of the Qadaffi regime was seriously wounded in a Libyan-government-instigated contract killing attempted by a former U.S. Special Forces soldier. The following July, another Libyan student was murdered in Utah by a fellow Libyan who was arrested as he attempted to return to Libya.

More serious indications of foreign terrorist activity in the United States surfaced in 1987 when a member of the renegade Palestinian Abu Nidal terrorist organization (a naturalized American citizen) was discovered living in Puerto Rico and in the process of establishing a network of terrorist cells and attendant support apparatus along the U.S. East Coast. He was extradited to Israel in 1989 on charges that he led an attack on a civilian bus three years before. Later that year, three Canadians of Lebanese descent were arrested by an alert Vermont police officer shortly after they crossed the border from Quebec en route to New York on a bombing mission. And, in possibly the most serious domestic terrorist incident until the Trade Center bombing, a Japanese terrorist, Yu Kikumura, sent to the United States by Colonel Qadaffi on a mission to avenge the retaliatory airstrike on Libya two years before, was apprehended on the New Jersey Turnpike before he could carry out a bombing attack in lower Manhattan.

The bombing of New York City's World Trade Center, in which six persons were killed and more than 1,000 injured, arguably marks a watershed in domestic terrorist trends. Until the February 1993 blast, many Americans regarded terrorism as something that happened elsewhere. Until the New York City incident, terrorism was a problem endemic to the already-violent Middle East and to the revolution-prone countries of Latin America that occasionally spilled over onto the streets of Paris, London, and Madrid. The New York City bombing not only shattered that complacency but possibly shattered America's sense of security as well. The attack demonstrated that Americans, though frequently the target of terrorists abroad, can no longer believe themselves immune to such violence within their own borders. Indeed, the reality of this threat was further underscored in June 1993 with the discovery of a plot by another group of Islamic militants to secure the release of the Trade Center terrorists through a campaign that involved plans to destroy two commuter tunnels and a bridge linking New Jersey to Manhattan, blow up the United Nations building, stage a forced-entry attack on the downtown building housing the FBI's New York field office, and assassinate various public officials, including Egyptian President Hosni Mubarak and U.S. Senator Alfonse D'Amato.

Despite our explicit statement of the FBI definition, it became clear from the responses that state and local law enforcement officials apply a looser and less-precise definition to what they consider terrorism. The survey respondents reported far more incidents than the FBI reported for the United States as a whole. For instance, racially or religiously motivated acts of violence, so-called "hate crimes" perpetrated by Skinheads and white supremacist gangs, were often cited, and counted, as terrorist incidents by state and local respondents. Similarly, other acts of apparent politically motivated violence, such as attacks on medical clinics performing abortions, were also cited by these respondents despite the absence of any incidents so defined by the FBI. What is more, respondents from municipalities of all sizes and from all regions responded affirmatively to questions about local terrorist threats in numbers greater than those the FBI reports. In other words, the "overreporting" of terrorism on the basis of the FBI definition was widespread and did not follow any identifiable pattern. Thus, although respondents were clearly departing from the FBI definition, and from the definition we intended, there may nevertheless be some uniformity to the definition of terrorism these diverse organizations applied.

Perhaps the main reasons for this divergence in definition is the rigorous analytical and legal process with which the FBI examines each incident before determining whether it is an act of terrorism or not. This involves detailed, ongoing investigation; the synthesis of often voluminous and disparate strands of information; and intense statutory scrutiny and analysis. The potential legal and political ramifications of a determination by the FBI that an incident is an act of terrorism are such that a significantly more cautious and conservative approach is embraced than that evident among the state and local jurisdictions surveyed as part of this study. This deliberative process, in which municipalities report suspected incidents to the FBI, and in which the FBI frequently determines that no act of terror occurred, may account for some of this discrepancy.

Poor communication, however, between federal, state, and local law enforcement authorities may also account for this disparity. In some municipalities, law enforcement personnel who are not specifically assigned to investigate terrorism or terrorist-related cases or who are generally unfamiliar with terrorism, for example, may not be aware that the FBI has been designated as the lead federal agency with authority to investigate acts of terrorism in the United States. Such law enforcement officials therefore may not know that all terrorist incidents and suspected terrorist incidents should be reported to the FBI. Alternatively, it may be that the incidents are reported to the FBI, which, upon further investigation, and in accordance with the aforementioned guidelines laid down for defining a criminal act as a terrorist incident, either reclassifies the incident as a suspected terrorist incident or determines that it is not in fact a terrorist incident.

Thus, one key finding of this study is that many state and local jurisdictions do not adhere to the official FBI definition of terrorism, either because they are unaware of the FBI guidelines for, or the rationale behind the process of, defining an incident as terrorism, or because of reasons that were not captured in the scope of this study.[3] Although it is clear that localities use a more expansive definition of terrorism than the FBI, it is equally clear that many state and local jurisdictions are indeed aware of the threat posed by terrorism in the United States, are alert to indications of that threat, and are attentive to criminal acts stemming from possible political motivation.

For the purpose of this study, given that state and local authorities consider a wider range of issues and activities to be terrorist acts than the FBI considers to meet the definition, we refer to the incidents that the states and municipalities report as terrorist ones. Hence, if those who answered the survey considered an incident a terrorist act, then that is how it is reported. Thus, throughout this document, the words "terrorism" and "terrorist" are imbued with the context imparted by the survey respondents, with the important caveat that these definitions may not, in many circumstances, conform to the FBI guidelines. This nomenclature, a departure from FBI convention, is appropriate for two reasons. First, because of the nature of the questions, we have little ability to determine which responses correspond to the FBI's criteria about terrorist events and which do not. Second, and more important, this research was designed to explicate terrorism and preparedness as it is viewed below the national level. Although this perception may vary widely from the official FBI definition, it is nonetheless important in understanding state and local law enforcement's perception of the problem.

State Law Enforcement Agencies

Nearly 80 percent (31 of 39) of the state law enforcement agencies responding to the survey noted the presence of an identified terrorist threat in their

---

[3]In our design of the survey instrument and attendant consultations with both the FBI and National Institute of Justice, we had not deemed it necessary to ask whether the respondents knew or were in fact aware of the FBI definition. In retrospect, this is an unfortunate oversight and a matter that deserves further research.

jurisdiction.[4] Moreover, nearly 90 percent of the respondents reported the presence of terrorist sympathizers and supporters within the state's borders.

The majority of states indicated the presence of right-wing terrorist groups. Some right-wing groups, such as the Ku Klux Klan, have been in operation for decades, whereas others, such as the Aryan Nations, are relative newcomers. Right-wing terrorist organizations are organized in many regions of the country, in cities both large and small, and have formed a loose nationwide network.

A number of the cities selected for case studies reported the presence of, or potential for, right-wing terrorism threats. The right-wing threat was perhaps most visible in Coeur d'Alene, Idaho, in the early 1980s when the Aryan Nations organization was active and apparently growing. The issue has since faded somewhat in Coeur d'Alene but has arisen elsewhere. Birmingham, Alabama, reports the presence of a group called the Aryan National Front. This group, with membership thought to be approximately 100, is known to have ties to the Ku Klux Klan but largely confines its activities to holding annual rallies.

Most state law enforcement organizations also noted the presence of issue-specific terrorist organizations. A list of the most prominent issue-specific groups with terrorist potential would include anti-abortion, environmental, and animal rights movements. Some issues groups, such as the anti-abortionists, appear to be making progress in organizing themselves at the national level; other issue groups, such as the animal rights organizations, are bound by little other than their common issues and objectives. Among the case study municipalities, Milwaukee, Whitehall (PA), and Coeur d'Alene (ID) report the presence of active anti-abortion groups. Miami is unique among the case study selections in that opposition to federal drug policy is a potentially large source of terrorism. Seattle has reported no violent incidents related to animal rights issues, but such groups are active in western Washington state.

Other types of terrorist organizations are not reported nearly as often as right-wing and issue-specific groups (see Table 3.1). Nearly 40 percent of the jurisdictions report ethnic terrorist organizations, and nearly 25 percent report left-wing terrorist groups. Among the case study locations, Puerto Rico and New York City are the locus of ethnic and emigre tensions. Puerto Rico is home to a

---

[4]Inexplicably, three of the eight respondents who answered "no" to the question "Have you identified any terrorist groups in your state?" went on to answer "yes" to questions about the presence of specific groups within the state. In all three cases the respondents answered yes to the presence of right-wing groups, and in one case answered yes to the presence of issue groups. Inspection of these three surveys revealed no clues behind the apparently conflicting nature of these three responses.

Table 3.1

State Law Enforcement Reports of State-Level Terrorist Groups
(N=39)

Group	No.	%
Right-wing	34	87
Left-wing	8	21
International	5	13
Ethnic	13	33
Issue-specific	23	59
Other	4	10

number of separatist and nationalist terrorist groups, many of which have also operated in New York City because of its large Puerto Rican population. Seattle is reported to be home to a number of left-wing organizations, although none have been implicated in violent acts. In the past, left-wing groups such as the Weather Underground committed terrorist acts in New York City, but more recently there have been no recorded cases. Ethnic and leftist terrorism threats, although significant, are relatively few in comparison to the figures for right-wing and issue-specific organizations.

Emergency Preparedness Organizations

Emergency preparedness organizations report results that are similar to those obtained from state law enforcement organizations. Sixty-five percent (24 of 37) of the responses from emergency preparedness organizations indicate that terrorist groups have been identified in their states. Again, right-wing (57 percent; 21 of 37) and issue-specific organizations (54 percent; 20 of 37) are most frequently mentioned, and ethnic groups are a strong third (35 percent; 13 of 37). Additionally, 57 percent (21 of 37) of the state emergency management organizations identified supporters of terrorist groups as residing in their states.

Municipal Law Enforcement Agencies

Approximately one-third of the municipal law enforcement agencies surveyed identified terrorist groups in their jurisdictions, and an additional one-third are aware that terrorist groups operate within their states. Additionally, 43 percent of the respondents reported that supporters and sympathizers of terrorist groups were active in their jurisdictions. Combined, a total of 83 percent (123 of 148) of local-level respondents noted the potential for terrorist threats in their states and municipalities. The percentages were approximately the same for both the targeted and population-based groups (see Table 3.2).

Table 3.2

Identification of Terrorist Groups at Municipal Level

Response	Population-Based Group (N=84)		Targeted Group (N=64)		Total (N=148)	
	No.	%	No.	%	No.	%
Yes, in jurisdiction	26	31	22	34	48	32
No	23	27	22	34	45	30
Yes, state level	32	38	18	28	50	34

NOTE: Columns do not add to 100 percent because categories are neither exhaustive nor mutually exclusive.

Of the 148 respondents, 91 (61 percent) reported right-wing terrorist groups at the state level; 26 (18 percent) reported left-wing terrorist groups; 22 (15 percent) reported international terrorist groups; 38 (26 percent) reported ethnic terrorist groups; and 84 (57 percent) reported issue-specific terrorist groups. Table 3.3 summarizes these results.

Table 3.3

Municipal Reports of State-Level Terrorist Groups
(N=148)

Group	No.	%
Right-wing	91	61
Left-wing	26	18
International	22	15
Ethnic	38	26
Issue-specific	84	57
Other	8	5

Regional Variations

According to FBI reports, actual incidents of terrorism have been disproportionately concentrated in Puerto Rico and the Western and Midwestern United States. The responses from the population-based portion of our sample indicate that municipalities' terrorist perceptions generally follow the same pattern. That is, 85 percent of Midwestern jurisdictions (17 of 20 from the population-based sample) and 79 percent of Western jurisdictions (23 of 29) report the presence of terrorist threats, whereas only 46 percent (6 of 13) Northeastern jurisdictions report the same. In one potentially significant break from the regional patterns the FBI reports, nearly 70 percent (15 of 22) of Southern jurisdictions report a terrorist presence, compared to zero incidents recorded by the FBI in the South between 1989 and 1993. Since our population-based sample excluded Puerto Rico, and since the FBI reports Puerto Rican terrorism separately, this finding cannot be related to Puerto Rican violence.

Instead, it may reflect Southern jurisdictions' concerns with abortion-related violence. An examination of Southern jurisdictions' reported terrorist threats indicates that the vast majority (18 of 23) consider their terrorist threat to be issue-related, a category that includes anti-abortion groups. To date, the FBI has not categorized any attacks against abortion clinics as terrorist-related. Table 3.4 summarizes these findings. Table 3.4 also indicates that Western, Southern, and Midwestern jurisdictions appear to be predominantly concerned with right-wing and issue-specific terrorist threats. In addition, the West reports the highest rates of left-wing and ethnic terrorist threats.

Table 3.4

**Distribution of Terrorist Organizations, by Type, Among the
Population-Based Sample**

| | Region and Number in Sample | | | |
Group	Midwest (20)	Northeast (13)	South (22)	West (29)
Right-wing	17	4	13	22
Left-wing	6	0	3	9
International	6	0	4	7
Ethnic	5	1	8	11
Issue-specific	14	4	15	18
Other	1	4	1	2
Total (reporting at least one group)	17	6	15	23

Reported Terrorist Threat and Municipality Size

In a pattern that will be evident across a number of dimensions of terrorism perceptions and preparedness, small and large cities differ in their interpretations of terrorism. Smaller cities, those with populations less than 100,000, are much less likely to report the presence of local terrorism threats than are large cities. Moreover, smaller cities are less likely to report a local problem, regardless of the individual terrorism category considered. As in the state-level samples, however, right-wing and issue-specific groups are most frequently mentioned as potential sources by smaller municipalities. This pattern holds, with appropriate caveats because of the small sample sizes, when the targeted sample, which is more likely to experience terrorist threats, is eliminated and only the population-based sample is considered. Table 3.5 summarizes municipal reports of terrorism threats.

In terms of the frequency of operations over the past decade, the municipalities report right-wing and issue-specific groups as having committed the most

Table 3.5

Reported Terrorism Threats, by Population Category

Population	Total Sample Population	Terrorist Groups in Jurisdiction		Population-Based Sample	Terrorist Groups in Jurisdiction	
		No.	%		No.	%
<10,000	27	3	11	15	1	6
10,000–50,000	41	10	24	18	10	28
50,001–100,000	22	5	23	15	4	26
100,001–250,000	21	12	57	17	9	53
250,001–500,000	13	7	54	6	3	50
500,001–1,000,000	19	8	44	11	3	30
1,000,000+	5	3	60	2	1	50
Total	148	48		84	31	

terrorist acts (see Table 3.6). Ethnic and emigre groups run a distant third. These patterns are consistent with trends noted in other research on terrorism in the United States.[5] The FBI attributes most U.S. acts of terrorism from 1988–1993 to Puerto Rican groups, and a smaller number to animal liberation and environmental groups. However, the 1993 *Terrorism in the United States* attributes two of the 12 incidents to right-wing groups, and nine to the Animal Liberation Front, a left-wing group. Other research documents significant right-wing activity that does not meet the FBI's definition of terrorism.[6]

Table 3.6

Frequency of Terrorist Acts, by Groups, as Reported by Municipalities

Terrorist Group	0	1–5	6–10	11–15	16–20	21+	Unknown
Reported Rate (%) in Overall Sample (N=148)							
Right-wing	66	18	8	3	1	2	1
Left-wing	93	5	0	0	0	<1	1
International	95	2	2	0	0	0	1
Ethnic	86	7	3	2	0	<1	1
Issue-specific	61	22	5	5	2	5	<1
Other	94	2	3	0	<1	0	<1
Reported Rate (%) in Population-Based Sample (N=84)							
Right-wing	70	14	10	1	1	1	2
Left-wing	93	5	0	0	0	0	2
International	93	4	1	0	0	0	2
Ethnic	83	6	5	2	0	1	2
Issue-specific	62	23	5	4	2	4	1
Other	93	1	4	0	1	0	1

NOTES: Missing responses are counted as 0 incidents. Percentage totals may not add across rows because of rounding.

---

[5]Bruce Hoffman, *Recent Trends and Future Prospects of Terrorism in the United States*, R-3618, (RAND: Santa Monica, Calif.), May 1988.

[6]Hoffman (1988).

Over the past five years, few municipal law enforcement agencies have been called upon to address terrorist incidents. Only 7 percent of the municipal forces surveyed report that there are ongoing investigations of terrorist groups within their jurisdictions. This finding is not surprising, given that the FBI has authority over, and responsibility for, investigation of all terrorist incidents in the United States and given that the FBI would assume jurisdiction over a case if a local investigation revealed a terrorism connection. Fifty-one percent (75 of 148) in the overall sample report no involvement with terrorism over the past five years, but 55 percent (46 of 84) in the population-based sample report no involvement; 26 percent (38 of 148) have participated in investigations of terrorist groups, as have 26 percent (22 of 84) from the population-based sample; 23 percent (34 of 148) have conducted surveillance of terrorist groups, but only 17 percent (14 of 84) among the population-based sample; 27 percent (40 of 148) have provided information about terrorist organizations to other agencies, a rate that drops to 21 percent (18 of 84) in the population-based sample; 26 percent have been placed on alert at the request of other agencies, a rate similar to the 23 percent rate (19 of 84) in the population-based sample; 8 percent (12 of 148) have been involved in prosecution, compared to 5 percent (4 of 84) in the population-based sample; 10 percent (15 of 148) involved with the collection of evidence, and 10 percent (8 of 84) in the population-based sample; and 1 percent (2 of 148) involved with scientific analysis of evidence for both groups.

Given the high percentages of municipalities that reported terrorist incidents, it is somewhat surprising that a relatively small number of municipalities have been involved in terrorism investigations over the past few years. One explanation might be that municipalities are constrained in their ability to undertake investigations of suspected terrorist organizations. In many cities, Seattle and New York are examples, police departments are forbidden from undertaking investigations of suspected or potential terrorist organizations solely on the basis of the group's political or social philosophy. Regulations such as these began to emerge with the revisions of domestic intelligence laws that occurred in the aftermath of Watergate and the revelation of the CIA's involvement in domestic spying.[7] One result has been an increase in the restrictions on investigatory and strategic law enforcement. In turn, this has led to a greater emphasis on tactical responses to terrorist incidents as they occur, rather than strategic responses designed to prevent terrorism incidents from developing.[8] More generally,

---

[7]See Sorrel Wildhorn, Brian Michael Jenkins, and Marvin M. Lavin, *Intelligence Constraints of the 1970s and Domestic Terrorism: Vol. I, Effects on the Incidence, Investigation, and Prosecution of Terrorist Activity*, N-1901-DOJ (RAND: Santa Monica, Calif.), December 1982, for a summary.

[8]This subject is addressed in Section 4, in the subsection entitled "Tactical and Intelligence Units." Counter-terrorism measures are activities that *respond* to terrorist acts once they have occurred; anti-terrorism measures are generally taken to mean activities that seek to *prevent* terrorist

many municipalities, except for the largest departments, cannot afford to staff intelligence divisions and consequently have only limited organizational and personnel resources to devote to anti-terrorism.

Summary

Right-wing and issue-specific groups are identified with the greatest frequency by all types of organizations. That is, all of the elements surveyed—state law enforcement, state emergency preparedness, and local law enforcement organizations—identified right-wing and issue-specific organizations as the two most prominent threat sources. These two types of terrorist organizations are not only the most frequently identified in terms of existence but also are most frequently identified as having committed specific acts of terrorism. These perceptions of terrorism are spread throughout the United States, in communities large and small.

Despite the near universal acknowledgment of the potential for terrorism, the rest of this report will reveal that there is no unanimity as to how to address the problem. Subsequent sections of this report will detail how the level of training, communications, coordination, and procedures vary from city to city and even from law enforcement agency to law enforcement agency within a given county. Clearly, law enforcement officers are aware of the potential threat from terrorism. But the potential immensity of terrorism, the sudden violence with which it may manifest itself, and the numerous forms in which the acts can be perpetrated are daunting issues which make preparedness difficult. As one member of the New York City Terrorism Task Force noted before the World Trade Center bombing, preparing for terrorism is difficult when "the whole city is a target."

---

acts. Tactical units are analogous to *counter*-terrorism operations because police tactical units respond to crime incidents. Intelligence and strategic units are analogous to *anti*-terrorism operations.

4. State and Local Preparedness

Overview

This section considers three elements of state and local preparedness against acts of terrorism: planning and resources, operational issues, and tactical issues. Analysis of planning and resources is designed to assess two main strategic issues. The first is whether law enforcement and emergency planning organizations are aware of the potential for terrorist acts in their communities and jurisdictions. If they are not aware of the possible threat of terrorism, it is unlikely that the capacity to respond will have been developed. Second, an analysis of planning and resources provides a better understanding of whether law enforcement and emergency planning organizations have the capacity to cooperate with external organizations in times of crisis. Thus, evaluation of planning and resources focuses on the availability of communication mechanisms between organizations, the frequency of contact and external review, and other matters relating to law enforcement and emergency preparedness organizations' relations to other institutions with terrorism responsibilities.

Whereas analysis of planning and resources assesses the community's terrorism awareness, analysis of procedures assesses the processes and protocols of terrorism preparedness. It is, in some sense, a measure of the *sufficiency* of preparedness. Thus, this section reports on the operating procedures that individual law enforcement and emergency preparedness organizations have developed to prevent, investigate, and prosecute terrorism incidents. Additionally, this section evaluates the links between the hierarchy of law enforcement elements with terrorist responsibilities, including questions of communities' access to state and federal organizations and resources.

Finally, analysis of tactical issues provides a basic measure of organizations' capacities to confront terrorism when it occurs. If a terrorist incident occurs, do enforcement agencies have the personnel and equipment on hand necessary to respond to an incident? Important issues to be examined here include which agencies provide the training, how often skills are upgraded and tested, and the proportion of organization members that receive such training.

Planning and Resources

Contingency planning is one major route through which organizations can judge the adequacy of their preparedness against terrorism. Indeed, the purpose of contingency planning is to identify available resources and identify ways those resources can be formed into an operational plan. Often, one major element of contingency planning is determining which organizations will bear responsibility for the various aspects of addressing a terrorist crisis. To this end, the FBI has conducted a detailed infrastructure vulnerability and protection program to identify and catalog key assets throughout the United States, develop liaison, and assist in contingency planning where necessary. The FBI's efforts are intended to facilitate the protection of the U.S. infrastructure.[1] This assessment has included surveys of all major commercial airports in the United States, nuclear power plants, and detailed response plans to a variety of nuclear, biological, and chemical terrorist scenarios.

An integral element of contingency planning is the coordination and liaison among agencies with terrorism responsibilities. Assessment of this segment reveals how frequently organizations are in contact with each other, the preparations and methods of information sharing, and the types of information that get shared.

Contingency Plans

Surprisingly, only 38 percent (n=15) of state law enforcement agencies have contingency plans for dealing with the threat of terrorism, compared to 52 (n=77) percent of the local agencies and nearly 56 percent (n=21) of the state emergency management organizations. The targeted and population-based samples are approximately equally likely to have contingency plans. Fifty-five percent (35 of 64) of the targeted respondents and 50 percent (42 of 84) of the population-based respondents reported contingency plans.

In the case of cities and counties, the likelihood of having a contingency plan increases with municipality size. About 63 percent (29 departments) of the 46 municipalities and counties with populations greater than 150,000 have terrorism contingency plans, whereas only approximately 46 percent (48) of the 102 jurisdictions with fewer than 150,000 do. Planning occurs at approximately the same rate for the targeted (47 percent, 20 of 43) and population-based (47 percent,

---

[1]See Federal Bureau of Investigation, Counter-Terrorism Section, Counter-Terrorism Planning Unit, *The FBI's Key Asset Infrastructure Program* (Washington, D.C.: U.S. Department of Justice, Federal Bureau of Investigation, n.d.).

28 of 59) samples in communities less than 150,000, but at a higher rate in the targeted sample (71 percent, 15 of 21) than in the population-based sample (56 percent, 14 of 25) for communities larger than 150,000. Again, this should be interpreted cautiously because of the small number of observations. This finding is not surprising, given that terrorist targets are more likely to be found in urban areas, and given that urban police forces are more likely to have a size and structure that permit contingency planning. Indeed, forces with less than 100 officers have contingency plans in only 39 percent of the cases (27 of 69), whereas forces with over 750 officers have terrorism plans 85 percent of the time (17 of 20).

Additionally, the likelihood of having contingency plans increases with the presence of high-risk targets such as weapons facilities, energy facilities, and military installations. When the targeted sample is eliminated and only the population-based sample is considered, the higher rate of planning remains. Thus, the presence of a sensitive facility appears to be correlated with increased planning. To some extent the correlation between the presence of sensitive facilities and contingency planning may be a function of population, since these facilities tend to be adjacent to urban areas that, as noted above, are more likely to have contingency plans. Overall, police forces with weapons plants in their communities develop contingency plans 66 percent of the time (25 of 38); forces with military facilities in their jurisdiction have them 65 percent of the time (42 of 65); and forces with energy facilities have them 64 percent of the time (16 of 25). Surprisingly, however, municipal forces in which nuclear power plants are located have terrorism contingency plans only 50 percent of the time (13 of 26). This rate is not only lower than the rate for other types of sensitive facilities but lower than the rate for the municipal sample as a whole. The apparent difference in planning rates for municipalities with nuclear facilities, however, may be an artifactual finding that is a result of the relatively small number of observations in the category.

Table 4.1 reveals that smaller municipalities are still less likely to create contingency plans, even in cases where they house sensitive facilities. Although clouded by the small number of observations in the cells, this pattern appears to hold for the population-based sample as well.

Organizations that receive federal funding are more likely to draw up contingency plans than municipalities that do not receive such funding. About 62 percent (n=85) of the municipalities that receive federal funds have contingency plans, compared to a 39 percent (n=57) contingency planning rate in communities that do not receive funds. The significance of this pattern is clouded by the fact that larger cities are more likely to receive federal funds. Thus, it is not clear whether it is the availability of federal funds or the size of the

Table 4.1

Contingency Planning Rate for Jurisdictions Housing Sensitive Facilities, by Population

Sensitive Facility	Population Size						Total No. of Facilities
	<100,000		100,001–500,000		>500,000		
	No.	%	No.	%	No.	%	
Total Sample							
Nuclear plants	10	53	0	0	4	80	26
Military installations	10	48	19	76	13	68	65
Weapons manufacturers	7	50	11	79	7	70	38
Energy plants	5	50	6	66	5	83	25
Population-Based Sample							
Nuclear plants	(a)	(a)	(a)	(a)	2	100	2
Military installations	5	36	13	87	6	54	40
Weapons manufacturers	3	43	7	88	2	40	20
Energy plants	1	33	3	60	1	100	11

[a]No observations.

municipality that leads to a greater degree of contingency planning in communities that benefit from federal funding.

The federal government also makes special counter-terrorism funds available. In our survey, municipalities in Michigan, Texas, Utah, Louisiana, Arkansas, and Georgia reported receiving federal funding dedicated to counter- and anti-terrorism purposes. Of these six, four have developed contingency plans and two have not.

Review of Contingency Plans

Of the 17 state law enforcement agencies with contingency plans, 11 reported that their contingency plans were reviewed by at least one other agency, and three reported that their plans were reviewed by three or more agencies. In the cases where contingency plans were reviewed, the FBI was the most frequent reviewing agency; the FBI inspected over 70 percent of the state law enforcement plans that were reviewed.

Emergency management organizations have their contingency plans reviewed more frequently than state-level law enforcement agencies. Of the 20 state emergency organizations that reported having contingency plans, 19 also reported that they were reviewed by the Federal Emergency Management Agency (FEMA). Additionally, 40 percent of the emergency management organizations' plans were reviewed by the FBI, 25 percent by other federal agencies, 45 percent by local agencies, and 90 percent by other state organizations. In fact, every state emergency management agency that reported having a contingency plan also reported having it reviewed by at least one other agency at the local, state, or federal level.

Despite the FBI's lead role in combatting terrorism, it reviews only approximately one-quarter of municipal contingency plans (20 of 77) overall, whereas other local agencies reviewed 47 percent of the municipalities' and counties' plans (36 of 77). Similarly, state agencies reviewed 35 percent of the local plans (27 of 77). Table 4.2 also reports the review process by the targeted and population-based groups. The findings suggest that the targeted communities, which were selected in part because they may offer richer terrorist targets, are generally more likely than the population-based respondents to avail themselves of contingency plan reviews at every level.

The examination of the review system highlights some potential weaknesses in the process. At issue is the strength of the connections between local and federal entities. Table 4.3 demonstrates that localities have very limited access to FBI and other federal review. About half of the municipalities and counties surveyed report having a terrorism contingency plan, but only approximately one-quarter of these plans are reviewed by the FBI—the organization with the primary responsibility for combatting terrorism in the United States. The largest single category of reviewers is other local agencies. A total of 35 percent of municipalities' and counties' contingency plans are reviewed by federal agencies, including the FBI and FEMA. Of this 35 percent total, 11 percent are reviewed only by the FBI, 9 percent are reviewed only by some other federal agency, and 16 percent are reviewed by both the FBI and another federal agency. A full 26 percent of the 77 municipalities with contingency plans (20 respondents) reported that no review whatsoever of their plans took place. These findings are summarized in Table 4.3.

Table 4.2

Review of County and Municipal Contingency Terrorism Plans
(N=77; 35 targeted and 42 population-based)

Reviewing Agency	% of Total Plans Reviewed	% of Targeted Plans Reviewed	% of Population-Based Plans Reviewed
FBI	26	26	19
Other federal agencies	25	25	14
State agencies	35	35	24
Other local agencies	47	57	38

NOTE: Column totals sum to more than 100 percent because of multiple reviews.

Table 4.3

Distribution of Contingency Plan Reviewing Agencies
(in percent)

	% with Plans	% with Plans That Are Reviewed by:						
		FBI	Other Federal	State	Local	Local Only	All Four[b]	None
Municipal LEAs (N=148)	52	26	25	35	47	12	6	26
State LEAs (N=39)	36	43	21	36	21	14	7	42[a]
Emergency Organizations (N=37)	54	35	90	80	35	0	10	0

[a]Includes one review listed as other.
[b]FBI, other federal, state, local.

The need for external review arises, in part, because many agencies intend their contingency plans to be used by other local, state, and federal agencies. When asked if the contingency plans were for single or multiagency use, 62 percent (48 of the 77 communities with plans) of the local plans were for use by other local agencies, 35 percent (27) by federal agencies, and 40 percent (31) by state law enforcement agencies. Similarly, the state agency plans included local agencies 61 percent of the time (9 of 15 cases), federal 46 percent (7 cases), and other state agencies 54 percent (8 cases) of the time.

Smaller cities and counties appear to differ from larger cities and counties in terms of their access to FBI review of contingency plans. That is, of the municipalities with contingency plans, small counties' and cities' are reviewed by the FBI in significantly lower proportions, both in the population-based and targeted samples. Table 4.4 summarizes this finding.

Equally surprisingly, municipalities with sensitive facilities such as nuclear power plants, military installations, and weapons manufacturers are no more likely to have their contingency plans reviewed than all municipalities taken as a whole.

Table 4.4

FBI Review of Contingency Plans, by Municipality Population

Size of Population	Reviewed by FBI (N=77)		Targeted (N=35)		Population-Based (N=42)	
	No.	%	No.	%	No.	%
<100,000	5	13	4	24	1	5
≥100,001	15	38	8	53	7	29

Cooperation and Liaison Among Agencies

One other important measure of access to federal terrorism agencies is the frequency of meetings and information exchanges between the institutions with terrorism responsibilities. Forty percent of the municipalities (59 of 148) report never having contact with federal agencies over terrorism issues. As across many other dimensions of terrorism preparedness, size appears to be a factor in liaison with federal agents. Only 7 percent of the forces with 500 (2 of 28) or more officers report never meeting with federal authorities over terrorism matters. In contrast, more than 53 percent of the forces with fewer than 100 officers (36 of 69) report never meeting with federal authorities. Federal authorities point out that liaison and review services are available, but that many municipalities fail to utilize them. Of course, this form of direct liaison through training or other law enforcement community interactions is dependent, to some extent, on the size of an organization's budget, a factor that often precludes agencies from smaller communities from taking advantage of such opportunities. Also, many cities, even those with populations greater than 100,000, are more than 100 miles from the nearest federal office. These budget and geographic constraints suggest that alternative forms of liaison and review, including teleconferencing and electronic document submission, may be necessary.

The police and sheriff forces of Kootenai County and Coeur d'Alene, Idaho, stand as exceptions to smaller municipalities' lack of cooperation and liaison with federal and state agencies. Coeur d'Alene, which has a population of just over 20,000, is located in Kootenai County. Much of Coeur d'Alene's and Kootenai County's preparedness for terrorism can be attributed to the small neighboring town of Hayden Lake. Hayden Lake is home to the Aryan Nations, an extremist, Neo-Nazi, white supremacist group. This group has been the subject of numerous law enforcement investigations, arising in part from its participation in annual conferences of white supremacists from throughout the United States, Canada, and abroad, and from the violent activities of splinter groups such as "The Order" (also known as "Silent Brotherhood II").

Kootenai County maintains a sheriff force of 100 officers, which includes a Special Response Team of 10 officers. The city police department has 44 officers and houses its own terrorism unit. Both agencies have received FBI field and in-house training as well as anti- and counter-terrorism training in other programs. Additionally, both organizations have participated in joint training exercises with the FBI. The California Special Training Institute has conducted special training sessions in Coeur d'Alene for local and state agencies, and a former Under Sheriff of the Kootenai County Sheriff's Department has developed a training program that is given throughout the Northwest. Coeur d'Alene's two municipal law enforcement agencies hold monthly meetings with the Bureau of Alcohol, Tobacco and Firearms (BATF), the Idaho Department of Law Enforcement, and Idaho Bureau of Narcotics, and law enforcement agencies from Spokane, Washington.

Many of the larger cities have developed extremely close relations with federal authorities over terrorism. Among the case study cities, both New York and Miami (Dade County, Florida) are participant cities in the FBI's regional joint task force program.[2] These programs, it should be noted, are extremely costly to organize, staff, and maintain given that the FBI pays overtime to local law enforcement officers serving on them and provides cars, office space, specialized equipment, and other support from a general services budget.

Miami established the Miami Joint Task Force on Terrorism in September 1989, largely in response to the high level of drug-related and anti-Castro violence the community experienced in the 1980s. The Miami Task Force is the youngest in the sample of case studies. In addition to having officers from the local law enforcement agencies (Dade County Sheriff and Miami Police), it includes officials from the Florida Department of Law Enforcement (FDLE), Florida National Guard, police department representatives from other counties, and numerous federal representatives, including authorities from the Immigration and Naturalization Service (INS); BATF; Internal Revenue Service (IRS); Central Intelligence Agency (CIA); the Border Patrol, Customs Department, State Department, Secret Service, and the U.S. Marshals Service.

Miami Task Force members report that there is excellent communication among the members and between the members' respective agencies. Individual members praise the task force for the rapid turnaround it provides on file and information requests for their own agencies. As a matter of routine, task force members analyze and disseminate information and transmit it back to the participating agencies. In the smaller adjacent jurisdictions that do not have members on the task force, liaison officers are designated to provide communication links.

Operational Issues

Emergency Management Agencies

State emergency management organizations were asked to report on their preparedness and ability to respond to acts of terrorism. Of the state emergency

---

[2]The other cities with joint task forces are Boston, Chicago, Denver, Houston, Los Angeles, Newark, Philadelphia, and San Diego.

management organizations that responded to this question, 58 percent (21 of 36) reported the existence of guidelines for responding to terrorism.

Interestingly, only two of 16 emergency organizations had developed response guidelines before 1987. The majority of respondents noted that their guidelines were developed in 1991 and 1992. The relative flurry of guideline planning that occurred in 1991 and 1992 can probably be attributed to the Gulf War and the consequent heightening of terrorist-related tensions during this period. One-third of the emergency management organization respondents reported that the threat of terrorism in 1993 was greater than in 1988. Additionally, 30 percent of the respondents reported that the threat of terrorism during the Gulf War had a major effect on their agency.

State and Local Law Enforcement Agencies

Law enforcement agencies at the state and local levels were asked a slightly different question about guidelines than were state emergency management organizations. Law enforcement organizations were asked about the existence of guidelines for the investigation of, rather than response to, terrorism threats.

State law enforcement agencies reported having state guidelines for the investigation of terrorism in 20 percent of the cases (8 of 39). These guidelines were developed between 1980 and 1991. Twenty-one percent of municipal law enforcement departments reported having terrorism investigation guidelines (30 of 148). The majority of these guidelines were developed after 1985. Only one municipality reported having developed guidelines before 1979.

In the population-based sample, the majority of investigation guidelines have been implemented in the South. The low rate of planning in the Northeast is consistent with the lower rates of perceived terrorism in the Northeast. The growth in the number of communities with guidelines in western parts of the country coincides with the growth in right-wing, white supremacist violence in these regions.[3] Idaho, for example, emerged as the center of Aryan Nation activity during the mid 1980s. Increased use of guidelines in southern communities may reflect increases in abortion-related tensions. In the latter stages of the 1985–1992 period, international terrorism emerged as a more prominent threat because of the Gulf War. Most municipalities (86 percent) report, however, that the Gulf War had little effect on their organizations. Thus,

---

[3]For more on the growth in these forms of domestic terrorism, see Hoffman (1988) and James Ridgeway, *Blood in the Face: The Ku Klux Klan, Aryan Nations, Nazi Skinheads and the Rise of a New White Culture* (Thunder's Mouth Press: New York), 1990.

it is not clear how much of the increase in contingency planning that occurred in 1990 and 1991 can be attributed to Gulf War fears. Table 4.5 summarizes the population-based sample's guideline development.

Table 4.5

Investigation Guidelines Among Population-Based Respondents, by Year and Region

Year Developed	Midwest	Northeast	South	West	Total
1970–1974	0	0	0	0	0
1975–1979	1	0	1	0	2
1980–1984	1	2	0	0	3
1985–1989	1	0	2	2	5
1990–present	0	0	5	0	5
Total	3	2	8	2	15

Development of Guidelines

The vast majority—87 percent—of municipal terrorism investigation guidelines were developed locally (26 of the 30 respondents). In the remaining four cases, respondents listed individuals' names so that a determination about local development could not be made. Responsibility for development varied, but most guidelines were devised by local police and sheriff department administrations, Special Weapons and Tactics (SWAT) commanders, special operations divisions, criminal intelligence (or investigation) divisions, or planning bureaus. In one case, the local prosecutor's office drew up the guidelines.

Only three jurisdictions reported the participation of non-local entities in the development of terrorism investigation guidelines, and only two reported federal assistance. One of the jurisdictions reporting federal assistance in developing guidelines was San Juan, Puerto Rico. San Juan has one of the highest levels of reported terrorist activities because several Puerto Rican nationalist and separatist organizations operate within its borders.

Two law enforcement organizations are tasked with terrorism duties in Puerto Rico. The Police of Puerto Rico, which is a state-level organization, has jurisdiction over terrorist events. Local organizations, such as La Guardia of San Juan, report directly to the Police of Puerto Rico. The FBI is the second major organization with terrorism responsibilities in Puerto Rico. Together, the Police of Puerto Rico and the FBI have established detailed procedures for the investigation, collection, and analysis of terrorist information. The FBI trains Puerto Rican police in federal crime procedures for the investigation of crime and bomb cases because, historically, many of such incidents have involved federal targets. Extensive training in federal procedures is regarded as vital because it aids in the prosecution of terrorism cases.

Intelligence is routinely shared between the Puerto Rican national police and the FBI. The free exchange of information is regarded as vital among the members of the law enforcement community in Puerto Rico. In particular, the flow of information helps protect the undercover agents and informants who are used extensively to augment intelligence files and operations.

In the event of a terrorist incident, the agencies jointly determine the division of responsibilities. Evidence is first sent to the police laboratories for analysis and then forwarded to the FBI. In cases of overlapping legal authority, jurisdiction is determined on the basis of the facts, including where the case might best be tried.

San Juan's terrorism procedures differ substantially from those of the Whitehall, Pennsylvania, police force. Whitehall is a small community of approximately 15,000 bordering Allentown. With a force of 39 members, Whitehall has provided seven officers with tactical training. Counter-terrorism is included in the tactical training, but the emphasis of the program is on basic tactical training such as defensive techniques and firearms handling. Members of the Whitehall Police Department receive no training in anti-terrorism.

In the event of a terrorism emergency, the Whitehall police would contact the Pennsylvania State Police. Beyond those arrangements for handling emergencies, Whitehall has designated its chief investigator as the primary liaison with the Pennsylvania State Police and the FBI. Lehigh County, in which Whitehall is located, sponsors a monthly meeting for all county police agencies and the FBI.

Terrorism Units

Only 35 percent (52 agencies) of the municipalities surveyed have specialized terrorism units. However, municipal and county police forces that have terrorist units are much more likely to indicate the presence of a terrorist threat in the local jurisdiction. Over 80 percent of the organizations with terrorist units reported the presence of a terrorist threat in the local jurisdiction and almost 90 percent of the same organization recognized a threat at the state level. In contrast, only 32 percent of the municipal and county forces without terrorist units identified local threats, and only 60 percent recognized a threat at the state level.

Survey respondents report that their terrorism units hold a wide variety of terrorism-related responsibilities. Most—about 80 percent (41 of 52)—of the special units are tasked with maintaining liaison with other local agencies. Other primary responsibilities include intelligence gathering, providing resources to other law enforcement agencies, and analyzing and disseminating data and analysis. Smaller numbers of the special forces have the responsibility of providing training for other agencies (36 percent, 19 departments), providing logistical support to other agencies (48 percent, 25 departments), and investigating specific terrorist incidents (38 percent, 20 departments).

Tactical and Intelligence Units

That terrorism units are assigned responsibility for investigating specific incidents with relatively low frequency is not surprising, given that many of the special terrorism units are tactical, rather than intelligence or strategic.[4] In practical terms, tactical units have the responsibility of responding to and controlling specific, crisis incidents as they emerge. In contrast, intelligence and strategic divisions and units devote a portion of their resources to surveillance, analysis, and investigation in an attempt to catch terrorism threats before they become active, as well as in an effort to solve them after they occur. To draw an analogy, tactical operations are the fireman of the terrorism world; intelligence and strategic operations are the fire safety inspectors.

Most of the terrorist units reported in the survey are housed in tactical units. Twenty cities report that their terrorism teams are based in SWAT units or other clearly identifiable tactical groups. In contrast, 15 cities report that their terrorism units are based in intelligence divisions. When these organizations are stratified by population, it becomes clear that terrorism units tend to be tactically oriented in smaller cities and a mixture of tactical and intelligence in larger cities. Of 13 cities with terrorist units and with population less than 100,000, ten have placed their terrorism groups in tactical groups. In larger cities, terrorism units are very nearly evenly split between tactical and intelligence units; six in the former and seven in the latter.

The distribution of terrorism into tactical and intelligence units is largely explainable by two factors. First, intelligence units are more expensive to

---

[4]Again, counter-terrorism measures are activities that *respond* to terrorist acts once they have occurred, whereas anti-terrorism measures are generally taken to mean activities that seek to *prevent* the execution of terrorist acts. Tactical units are analogous to *counter*-terrorism operations because police tactical units respond to crime incidents. Intelligence and strategic units are analogous to *anti*-terrorism operations.

maintain and difficult to justify, particularly in small municipalities where there are likely to be fewer manpower resources and fewer organized crime threats. Large cities face more intense pressure to address crimes as they happen, an argument for a tactical approach, but at the same time are likely to face more complex criminal environments that would warrant a strategic approach. Second, even in the larger cities where an intelligence-based approach is perhaps more justifiable, is it not always possible to maintain, particularly if law enforcement budget resources are scarce.

Birmingham Alabama, located in Jefferson County, is one example of a police department where it has not proven possible to locate the terrorism unit in an intelligence division. In fact, the Birmingham Police Department has no intelligence unit or division, and the counter-terrorism unit resides within a Tactical Operations Unit. Similarly, the Jefferson County Sheriff's Department's counter-terrorism unit resides in the organization's SWAT unit. Like the Birmingham police, Jefferson County has no intelligence unit or division, although it did maintain one until the late 1970s when budgetary constraints forced the unit's closure.

This unit has 37 members, and its primary responsibilities are freeway patrol, mounted patrol, hit-and-run investigations, and bomb squad investigations. This unit has received training from the FBI both at the national academy and in the field. Additional training has been provided by the Department of Energy, the United States Army, the Secret Service, the Federal Aviation Administration, and out-of-state law enforcement organizations. The Tactical Operations Unit provides an advanced SWAT training school each year which is attended by approximately 60 people.

Among other tasks, an intelligence unit would cultivate intelligence sources, coordinate intelligence information, act as a repository of intelligence information, and disseminate intelligence to tactical and strategic divisions. One consequence of not having an intelligence unit is that information gathered on terrorist organizations tends to be situation-specific. Once a case is closed, no attempt is made to keep files current because other active cases and responsibilities take precedent. The department's ability to address potential terrorism threats proactively is thus limited. Department officials noted this as a significant weakness in department operations.

Tactical Issues

Training

Another assessment of terrorism preparedness is the amount of training that takes place. In particular, two types of training, anti-terrorism and counter-terrorism, are relevant when considering preparedness issues. Anti-terrorism is defined as measures taken to prevent terrorism acts from occurring. Anti-terrorism thus primarily consists of physical security measures designed to thwart the execution of terrorist acts. In contrast, counter-terrorism involves monitoring and analyzing terrorist threats, as well as responding to terrorist acts once they have been committed.

Counter and anti-terrorism training is provided by 23 percent of local law enforcement organizations (34 departments). An additional 30 percent (44 departments) report that special counter- and anti-terrorism training is provided by the state. Other training is provided by the FBI, the Bureau of Alcohol, Tobacco and Firearms, the Department of Energy, the U.S. Army, and private agencies and professional associations. When duplications are eliminated, 72 percent of the local departments (107 of 148) received terrorism training from one organization or another.

In some cases, the training is coordinated at the state level. In Miami, for example, the Florida Department of Law Enforcement is responsible for regulating the certification of law enforcement and corrections officers. Thus, before joining the Miami Task Force, FDLE and local officers are required to receive additional training in federal terrorism procedures, including the investigation of terrorism groups. Members of the task force attend at least one FBI course in terrorism. Additionally, task force members attend anti-terrorism programs sponsored by the Secret Service and the State Department's Dignitary Protection School, as well as various in-house training programs.

Coffey County, Kansas, is notable because its counter-terrorism training was provided by a private agency. Coffey County is the home of Wolf Creek Nuclear Station. In 1972, before the construction of the station, the Coffey County Sheriff's office was manned by two officers. With the construction of Wolf Creek, however, the force has grown to nine officers, four of whom make up the Strategic Response Team. The Strategic Response Team has received extensive counter-terrorism training from Wolf Creek Security Force, a private organization that provides security for the nuclear facility.

Initial training for Coffey County forces consisted of an intensive two-week course, which included day and night exercises of various scenarios. The exercises used National Guard units and their explosives specialists to add realism and to provide needed equipment, such as helicopters. The Kansas Highway Patrol and the FBI participate in these exercises, which have been held twice since the opening of the plant in 1986, as well.

County officers supplement their training with semiannual tours of the plant to keep up to date on the layout of the facility and to be briefed on any changes in the security plan. The Kansas Bureau of Investigation and the Burlington Police Department make yearly tours of the plant, although neither receives counter-terrorism training.

Additional state and local organizations are involved in emergency preparedness exercises, which are also conducted twice a year. The emergency preparedness exercises include the same agencies that receive the counter-terrorism training, as well as the fire department, the health department, the road and bridge department, and the agricultural cooperative. FEMA and the Nuclear Regulatory Commission monitor these drills. The county is ranked on the basis of its response and has consistently been given one of the highest evaluations in the country.

Related Operational Units

Another perspective on terrorism training is the presence of related units that have some relationship to terrorism issues. For example, gang units and organized crime units might well have skills and training that relate to terrorism issues. Of the 92 local departments reporting that they do not have special terrorism units, 22 also report that they have no narcotics, gang, organized crime, white collar crime, or other specialized crime units. Similarly, of the 42 agencies reporting that they receive no terrorism training, 14 report that they have none of the above-listed specialized units.

Scale and Frequency of Training

Of the 113 departments that receive terrorism training, more than 35 percent (39 departments) have five or fewer officers who receive the preparation. Eighty-three percent (94 of 113) of the departments have 20 or fewer officers trained in anti- and counter-terrorism.

Approximately 41 percent of the terrorism training received by local departments is done on either a one-time or as-needed basis. Nearly as much of the training,

38 percent, is repeated every one to two years. The balance of the municipalities, about 21 percent, refresh their terrorism training every three to five years.

One frequent avenue of augmenting counter- and anti-terrorism skills is the conduct of joint training exercises. Approximately half of the organizations with terrorism units and approximately 41 percent of the organizations whose personnel have terrorism training have participated in joint training exercises with the FBI.

Training Procedures

A wide range of agencies participate in the training of local officers. The FBI is most often mentioned as a training source, both at the FBI National Academy and in the field. The states are the next most frequently mentioned training source, followed by professional organizations and private sources, the Army, local police academies, the BATF, and the Department of Energy. Of the cities reporting state training, 50 percent of those who received specialized terrorism training assisted in designing and conducting the training.

5. Conclusions, Policy Implications, and Future Research Areas

Survey Findings

The survey results indicate that a sizable majority of state and municipal law enforcement organizations consider terrorism, or the threat thereof, to be a problem. Of particular note is that many state and local law enforcement organizations consider a wider range of activities and acts terrorist, or potentially terrorist, than the FBI. Thus, although official FBI terrorist statistics point to low levels of terrorist activity, attribute many recent terrorist activities to Puerto Rican nationalists, and until 1993 did not count many threatening acts by organizations such as the Skinheads as terrorist, states and municipalities are equally adamant in identifying right-wing (Neo-Nazi, anti-Semitic, anti-federalist) and issue-specific (anti-abortion, animal rights, environmentalist) organizations as the most threatening actual and potential terrorist sources.

While in agreement that terrorism presents a challenge to law enforcement organizations, states and municipalities diverge in their approaches to the problems. The findings demonstrate compellingly that smaller jurisdictions, which may house sensitive facilities such as nuclear power plants, communications nodes, and so forth, have different approaches to terrorism preparedness than large cities. These differences are evident in areas ranging from development of terrorism guidelines and contingency plans, to training and operations.

Case Studies

In addition, the case studies revealed how different jurisdictions have adapted to the threat of terrorism and which anti- and counter-terrorism programs have been employed by these jurisdictions. In general, the case study results parallel the survey findings but provide additional detail. A variety of communities, ranging from Kootenai County and Coeur d'Alene, Idaho, to Miami and New York City, report very successful terrorism relations with the FBI. Miami and New York City host joint regional task forces which are an effective, but expensive, mechanism for addressing terrorism. Kootenai County and Coeur d'Alene, too, have cultivated close relations with the FBI over terrorism, largely because of their proximity to the right-wing extremists in nearby communities. As communities of differing sizes, confronting terrorist threats of differing origins, begin to develop terrorism communication and liaison mechanisms, Miami, New York City, Kootenai County, and Coeur d'Alene may serve as useful models.

San Juan, Puerto Rico, and Whitehall, Pennsylvania, provide contrasting paths for addressing terrorism emergencies and developing terrorism investigation guidelines. San Juan has developed extensive procedures because of its indigenous terrorist problem. One consequence is that San Juan law enforcement organizations enjoy close contact with the FBI. In contrast, Whitehall, which confronts a nascent anti-abortion movement, relies on the Pennsylvania State Police for tactical support in terrorism emergency situations. The procedures developed in the two communities suggest that a community's size, its resources, and the nature of the terrorism threats it confronts will influence both the strategic and tactical law enforcement response. In addition, the resource and geographic constraints that many smaller communities face, and the prevalence of terrorism concerns in such communities, suggest that innovative forms of liaison and review, including teleconferencing and electronic document submission, may be appropriate.

Birmingham, Alabama, illustrates the tradeoff that exists between tactical and strategic responses to terrorism. Birmingham authorities report that they would like to maintain a more proactive, preventive response to terrorism threats but are constrained by the expense associated with collecting, analyzing, and retaining terrorism-related intelligence. Seattle and New York report that they are constrained in their ability to investigate suspected or potential terrorist organizations on the basis of the group's political or social philosophy. Such constraints have also hampered the strategic and intelligence environment. Both communities' resource constraints and the changing intelligence environment suggest that the FBI may wish to examine the tradeoff between tactical (training, incident investigation) and strategic (planning, intelligence) assistance. Clearly, communities have needs in both areas, although it is far from clear which is more urgent.

In sum, sharing FBI intelligence and investigation findings with localities is considered very useful, and municipalities highly value their communication with federal authorities. Localities are interested in adopting a strategic approach in which intelligence, planning, and advance preparation are used to combat terrorism, but they lack the resources in many cases to maintain this more expensive approach. A variety of successful terrorism preparedness formulas exist, ranging from extensive cooperation and support with the FBI to responses in which the communities themselves assume a greater share of the burden.

Future Research Areas

A number of findings emerged during the survey and case studies, as well as in the aftermath of the World Trade Center bombing and the siege in Waco, Texas, that suggest future research. These future research issues can be broken out into the following broad categories: intelligence, border security, training, monitoring and evaluation, technology developments, community relations, and conferences.

Preventive Intelligence

The potential role of intelligence in preventing terrorism emerged strongly with some of the case study respondents and also appeared in the survey findings. Numerous changes in the intelligence environment have occurred in recent years, including court rulings on searches and seizures, surveillance, and investigative statutes. A study that examined the role of intelligence as a preventative device in light of these changes, and in light of the terrorist bombing of the World Trade Center, would prove invaluable.

Border Security

The porous nature of America's borders, the difficulties of controlling illegal immigration, and the smuggling of illicit goods and contraband have long been recognized as major problems and challenges. They have assumed new relevance in the wake of the World Trade Center bombing. One step toward improving border security might be to examine the strengths and weaknesses of cooperation between state, local, and federal authorities over border matters, particularly as they pertain to terrorism. Such a study would survey and audit state and local law enforcement cooperation and coordination with federal authorities in key urban areas such as San Diego and El Paso, as well as in more rural jurisdictions in Arizona and New Mexico. The goal of the project would be to make recommendations for a more comprehensive approach to ensuring border security.

Training

The FBI recently concluded a nationwide survey of critical infrastructure potentially attractive and/or vulnerable to terrorist attack. This project would take the results of that survey and investigate how well state and local law enforcement organizations are prepared to respond to attacks on the identified infrastructure in their jurisdictions. Again, the bombing of the World Trade Center and the massive emergency response by city, state, New York–New Jersey Port Authority, and federal authorities underscores the need for an evaluation of terrorism response capabilities.

Monitoring and Evaluation

How do individual state and local law enforcement agencies themselves monitor their own programs and training? How involved are federal agencies such as the FBI in these procedures? The survey findings presented here suggest that smaller jurisdictions may be at a disadvantage with respect to programs and training. Yet, resource limits at the municipal and federal levels may preclude establishing a national standard. Nevertheless, the need for such a standard should be examined in detail.

Technology Developments

In light of the siege in Waco, Texas, are there potential non-lethal technologies involving the use of force, eavesdropping, or surveillance that would assist law enforcement when confronted with similar dangerous situations? Are current communication devices state-of-the-art and adequate?

Community Relations

How can law enforcement relations with often closed, scared and, in many instances, isolated communities such as religious and messianic sects be affected and improved so that law enforcement can better respond to, and have fewer misunderstandings with, these groups? This project takes on particular relevance after the incident in Waco, and in light of the terrorism threats many smaller communities reported.

Conferences

A national conference to improve state, local, and federal cooperation in countering terrorism would bring together law enforcement officials from urban and rural areas, and from different functional areas (intelligence, investigation, SWAT, hostage negotiation) for the first, organized national conference designed not only to facilitate the exchange of information but to build greater national cooperation.

Appendix
A. Survey Instrument

DOMESTIC TERRORISM: NATIONAL ASSESSMENT OF STATE PREPAREDNESS

SECTION A: ABOUT YOUR ORGANIZATION

For the purposes of this survey our definition of terrorism is the unlawful use of force or violence against persons or property to intimidate or coerce a government, the civilian population, or any segment of either, to further political or social objectives.

A1. Is your department responsible for setting policy and developing emergency response and contingency plans for dealing with the threat of terrorism?

    1. Yes   6/
    2. No, ----->Who is responsible?   7-8/

                        _____

                        _____

A2. Do you have contingency plans for dealing with the threat of terrorism?

    1. Yes   9/
    2. No, GO TO Question A5.

A3. Have these contingency plans been reviewed by any of the following agencies? (Circle all that apply)

    1. FBI.   10/
    2. Other federal agencies.   11/
    3. State agencies.   12/
    4. Other local law enforcement agencies.   13/
    5. Other, please specify _____   14-15/

A4. Are these contingency plans designed for multi-agency use?
What other agencies are included? (Circle all that apply.)

1. No other agencies 16/
2. Local law enforcement 17/
3. State law enforcement 18/
4. Other state agencies 19/
5. Federal agencies 20/
6. Security agencies 21/
7. Other, please specify _____ 22-23/

A5. How often does your department meet or exchange information
on terrorism with other **county or municipal agencies**?

1. Once a week or more. 24/
2. Two or three times month.
3. Once every month or two.
4. A few times a year.
5. Annually.
6. Never.

A6. How often does your department meet or exchange information
on terrorism with **state agencies**?

1. Once a week or more. 25/
2. Two or three times month.
3. Once every month or two.
4. A few times a year.
5. Annually.
6. Never.

A7. How often does your department meet or exchange information
on terrorism with **federal agencies**?

1. Once a week or more. 26/
2. Two or three times month.
3. Every month or two.
4. A few times a year.
5. Annually.
6. Never.

GUIDELINES

A8. Does your **state** have defined guidelines for the investigation of terrorism?

    1. Yes
    2. No, GO TO Question A13.   27/

A9. Who developed the guidelines? _____   28-29/
_____
_____

A10. In what year were the guidelines developed?   19 |__|__| 30-31/

A11. How many times have these guidelines been modified?

    1. Never ----->GO TO Question A13.   32/
    2. Once
    3. Twice
    4. Three or more times.

A12. In what year were they last modified?   19 |__|__| 33-34/

A13. Does your **Department** have defined guidelines for the investigation of terrorism?

    1. Yes
    2. No, GO TO Question A18.   35/

A14. Who developed the guidelines? _____   36-37/
_____
_____

A15. In what year were the guidelines developed?   19 |__|__| 38-39/

A16. How many times have these guidelines been modified?

    1.   Never ----->GO TO Question A18.   40/
    2.   Once
    3.   Twice
    4.   Three or more times.

A17. In what year were they last modified?   19 |__|__| 41-42/

SPECIAL TRAINING

Anti-terrorism is defined as the prevention of terrorist acts primarily, but not exclusively, through physical security measures, while counter-terrorism is the collection and analysis of intelligence, developing contingencies and allocation of specific sources, both to anticipate terrorist acts and to respond to them once they have occurred.

A18. Is counter- or anti-terrorism covered in your Police Academy?

    1.   Yes   44/
    2.   No

A19. Does your state provide special training in counter- or anti-terrorism, other than the Academy?

    1.   Yes, ----> How many times a year? _____   45/
    2.   No, GO TO Question A21.   46-47/

A20. What role does your office play in this training? (Circle all that apply)

    1.   Designed the training agenda.   48/
    2.   Assist in designing the training agenda.   49/
    3.   Conduct the training.   40/
    4.   Assist in conducting the training.   51/
    3.   No role in this training.   52/

A21. How many people in your department have received special training in counter- or anti-terrorism? _____   53-55/

A22. Where did they receive this training? (Circle all that apply)

1.   Police Academy   56/
2.   State sponsored training course -- in state   57/
3.   State sponsored training course -- out of state   58/
4.   In-house training course   59/
5.   FBI National Academy   60/
6.   FBI, training in the field   61/
7.   Bureau of Alcohol, Tobacco, and Firearms   62/
8.   Department of Energy   63/
9.   U.S. Army   64/
10. Professional associations, fraternal organizations,
     informal working group or private agency;   65/
     Names _____
11. Other, please specify _____   66-67/

A23. How often do the personnel in your department receive
      special training in counter- or anti-terrorism?

1.   One time only.   68/
2.   Every year or two.
3.   Every three to five years.
4.   Other, please specify _____

                                              |__|__|__| 1-3/
                                              Card 02   4-5/

A24. Has your department participated in any **joint training
      exercises** with: (Circle all that apply.)

1.   FBI   6/
2.   State agencies -- in state   7/
3.   State agencies -- out of state   8/
4.   Other county or municipal agencies   9/
5.   U.S. Secret Service   10/
6.   DEA   11/
7.   Border Patrol   12/
8.   Department of Energy   13/
9.   Professional associations, fraternal organizations,
     informal working group or private agency;   14/
     Names _____
10. Private businesses   15/
11. Other, specify _____   16/
     _____   17-18/

TERRORISM UNIT

A25. Does your department have a special unit, section, group or
     person that is specifically concerned with terrorism?   19/

     1. Yes, -----> How many people are in this unit? _____   20-22/

     2. No, -----> Do you think you need such a special unit or
                    section?

                    1. Yes, GO TO Question A31.   23/
                    2. No, GO TO Question A31.

A26. What is the name of this unit or individual?_____   24-25/
     _____
     _____

A27. Which of the following activities describe the duties of
     this unit? (Circle all that apply)

     1. Intelligence gathering.   26/
     2. Analysis and dissemination of information.   27/
     3. Training for other law enforcement agencies.   28/
     4. Liaison with other law enforcement agencies.   29/
     5. Provide resources to other law enforcement agencies.   30/
     6. Provide intelligence to other law enforcement agencies.   31/
     7. Provide logistical support to other law enforcement agencies. 32/
     8. Liaison with federal agencies.   33/
     9. Investigate specific terrorist incidents.   34/

A28. Does this unit participate in formal groups, meetings or
     joint-task forces with federal, state, local or private
     agencies?

     1. Yes   35/
     2. No, GO TO Question A30.

A29. How often do they meet?

     1. Once a week.   36/
     2. Twice a month.
     3. Once a month.
     4. Quarterly.
     5. Twice a year.
     6. Once a year.

A30. Has this unit participated in any **joint training exercises** with: (Circle all that apply)

1.	FBI	37/
2.	State agencies -- in state	38/
2.	State agencies -- out of state	39/
3.	Other county or municipal agencies	40/
4.	U.S. Secret Service	41/
5.	DEA	42/
6.	Border Patrol	43/
7.	Department of Energy	44/
8.	Private businesses	45/
9.	Professional associations, fraternal organizations, informal working group or private agency; Names _____	46/
10.	Other, specify _____ _____	47-48/

A31. What other special units do you have in your department? (Circle all that apply)

1.	Narcotics	49/
2.	Gangs	50/
3.	Organized crime	51/
4.	White collar crime	52/
5.	Other, please specify _____	53-54/

SECTION B: THREAT ASSESSMENT

For our purposes, a terrorist incident is a violent act, or an act
dangerous to human life or property, in violation of the criminal laws
of the United States or of any state, to intimidate or coerce a
government, the civilian population, or any segment of either, to
further political or social objectives.

B1. Have you identified any terrorist groups in your jurisdiction?

    1. Yes   55/

    2. No

B2. Do you have any of the following terrorist groups located in your
     state? (This includes not only those who have committed acts of
     politically motivated violence, but also those who may have, or
     may be planning acts of politically motivated violence.)
     (Circle all that apply.)

    1. **Right Wing** (i.e., anti-federalist, racist, anti-semitic,   56/
        tax-resisting, etc.)

    2. **Left Wing** (i.e., revolutionary, Marxist-Leninist, Maoist,   57/
        Trotskyite, etc.)

    3. **International** (i.e., foreign terrorist groups, or groups   58/
        sponsored by foreign governments in the U.S.)

    4. **Ethnic/Emigre** (i.e., terrorist groups from ethnic or   59/
        resident emigre communities within the U.S.)

    5. **Issue Specific** (i.e., environmental, animal rights,   60/
        anti-abortion, etc.)

    6. Other, please specify _____   61-62/

B3. Are any identifiable supporters/sympathizers active in your
     jurisdiction?   65/

    1. Yes

    2. No |__|__|__| 1-3/
                         Card 03 4-5/

B4. In the last ten years, roughly how many incidents have been
     attributed to terrorist groups in your jurisdiction. Please give
     us your best estimate.

Number of incidents:

	0	1-5	6-10	11-15	16-20	Over 21	
1. Right Wing	1	2	3	4	5	6	6/
2. Left Wing	1	2	3	4	5	6	7/
3. International	1	2	3	4	5	6	8/
4. Ethnic/Emigre	1	2	3	4	5	6	9/
5. Issue Specific	1	2	3	4	5	6	10/
6. Other	1	2	3	4	5	6	11/

B5. How has your department been involved in any terrorist or
     terrorist-related incident in the last five years?
     (Circle all that apply)

    1. Not involved.   12/
    2. Investigation.   13/
    3. Surveillance.   14/
    4. Asked to provide information to other agencies.   15/
    5. Placed on alert, at the request of other agencies.   16/
    6. Prosecution.   17/
    7. Collection of evidence.   18/
    8. Scientific analysis.   19/
    9. Other, please specify _____   20-21/

B6. Are there any current investigations of terrorist groups
     in your department?

    1. Yes   22/
    2. No

B7. Do you coordinate terrorist investigations with Federal
     agencies?

    1. Yes   23/
    2. No

B8. What type of support have you received from Federal agencies
     for terrorist investigations? (Circle all that apply)

    1. Intelligence   24/
    2. Use of databases   25/
    3. Logistical support   26/
    4. Material support   27/
    5. Other, please specify _____   28-29/
           30-31/

B9. Which agencies do you coordinate with during terrorist
    investigations? (Circle all that apply.)

    1. FBI.   32/
    2. Department of Energy.   33/
    3. FAA.   34/
    4. Department of State.   35/
    5. United States Secret Service.   36/
    6. Department of Transportation.   37/
    7. United States Customs Service.   38/
    8. State law enforcement agencies.   39/
    9. Other state agencies.   40/
    10. International agencies.   41/
    11. State or local transportation agencies.   42/
    12. County or local law enforcement agencies.   43/
    13. Other, please specify _____   44-45/
                                                        46-47/

B10. How would you categorize your general working relationship with
     these Federal agencies at this time?

    1. Very good   ---   48/
    2. Good |-->GO TO Question B12.
    3. Average   ---
    4. Fair
    5. Poor

B11. What do you think could be done to improve this relationship?
    _____   49-50/
    _____   51-52/
    _____   53-54/
    _____
    _____
    _____
    _____
    _____
    _____

B12. Do you coordinate terrorist investigations with other local
     agencies?

    1. Yes   55/
    2. No

B13. In what way have you supported other local agencies in terrorist investigations? (Circle all that apply)

        1.   Intelligence   56/
        2.   Use of databases   57/
        3.   Logistical support   58/
        4.   Material support   59/
        5.   Other, please specify _____   60-61/
        6.   Other local agencies have provided support to your   62-63/
             Department.

B14. How would you categorize your working relationship with these local agencies?

        1.   Very good   ---
        2.   Good |-->GO TO Question B16.   64/
        3.   Average   ---
        4.   Fair
        5.   Poor

B15. What do you think could be done to improve this relationship?
        _____   65-66/
        _____   67-68/
        _____   69-60/
        _____
        _____
        _____
        _____
        _____
        _____

                                            |__|__|__| 1-3/
                                            Card 04   4-5/

B16. Do you coordinate terrorist investigations with state agencies?

        1.   Yes   6/
        2.   No

B17. What type of support have you received from state agencies for terrorist investigations? (Circle all that apply)

        1.   Intelligence   7/
        2.   Use of databases   8/
        3.   Logistical support   9/
        4.   Material support   10/
        5.   Other, please specify _____   11-12/
                                                                    13-14/

B18. How would you categorize your working relationship with these state agencies?

    1. Very good   ---   15/
    2. Good |-->GO TO Section C, page 13.
    3. Average   ---
    4. Fair
    5. Poor

B19. What do you think could be done to improve this relationship?

    _____ 16-17/
    _____ 18-19/
    _____ 20-21/
    _____
    _____
    _____
    _____
    _____

SECTION C: RISK ASSESSMENT

Vulnerability is defined here as a condition that can be exploited by an adversary in a hostile action. Threat assessment is a judgement, based on available intelligence, law enforcement and open source information, of the actual or potential threat posed by an adversary.

C1. Has your department conducted a threat assessment of the vulnerabilities of key public, private, governmental and military facilities, and infrastructure, either:

		YES	NO	
A.	Specifically for terrorism	1	2	22/
B.	For a range of contingencies including terrorism	1	2	23/

C2. In what year was the assessment completed?   19|__|__| 24-25/

C3. Was a threat assessment completed by a state agency or department?

1. Yes, name of agency _____   26/
27-28/

Year: 19|__|__| 29-30/

2. No

C4. Do you have any of the following located in your jurisdiction? (Circle all that apply)

1. Military installation.   31/
2. Nuclear power plant.   32/
3. Department of Energy nuclear facility, such as a research laboratory, production factory, or storage area.   33/
4. Weapons manufacture or storage.   34/

C5. Are there any other facilities in your jurisdiction that would make your state a more attractive target to terrorist attack, as opposed to a neighboring jurisdiction?

1. Yes, -----> What are they?_____   35/
2. No   _____   36-37/
_____   38-39/

SECTION D: THREAT ENVIRONMENT

D1. In your opinion, is the threat of terrorism now greater,
     less, or about the same in the United States than it was
     five years ago?

                                                                    40/
     1. Greater --->Why? _____   41-42/
                     _____   43-44/
                     _____
                     _____
                     _____

     2. Less
     3. About the same.

D2. What impact, if any, did the threat of terrorism during the
     the Gulf War last year have on your agency?

     1. A great deal of impact.   45/
     2. Little impact.
     3. No impact.

D3. Were you satisfied with the sources and quality of information
     on the possible terrorist threat in the U.S. during the Gulf war?

     1. Yes   46/
     2. No, why not? _____   47-48/
                     _____   49-50/
                     _____

D4. The following is a list of possible sources of information
     pertaining to terrorism. How useful have you found these sources
     to be?

		Never Used	Not Useful	Somewhat Useful	Very Useful	
1.	FBI unclassified reports.	1	2	3	4	51/
2.	FBI classified reports.	1	2	3	4	52/
3.	Other federal agencies.	1	2	3	4	53/
4.	State agencies.	1	2	3	4	54/
5.	Other local jurisdictions.	1	2	3	4	55/
6.	The media.	1	2	3	4	56/
7.	Professional law enforcement publications.	1	2	3	4	57/
8.	Risk assessment services or publications.	1	2	3	4	58/
9.	Books, journals, periodicals, non-law enforcement publications.	1	2	3	4	59/
10.	Radical publications, other "alternative" literature.	1	2	3	4	60/
11.	Informants, sources on the street.	1	2	3	4	61/
12.	Other _____	1	2	3	4	62/
						63-64/

62

D5. The Attorney General has designated the FBI as the lead federal law enforcement agency in the fight against terrorism and there are counter-terrorism personnel in each field office. Have you or any of your department interacted with these counter-terrorism personnel to discuss the threat of terrorism in your jurisdiction?
(Circle all that apply.)

1. Meetings.   65/
2. Telephone conversations.   66/
3. Corresponded or received information.   67/
4. No contact.   68/

|__|__|__| 1-3/
Card 05   4-5/

D6. In the United States, terrorists have not assaulted major installations to date. How likely do you think the possibility that terrorists will in the next 10 years, attack:

	Very likely	Somewhat likely	Not very likely	Not likely	
Commercial nuclear plants.	1	2	3	4	6/
Military installations.	1	2	3	4	7/
DOE nuclear installations.	1	2	3	4	8/
Telecommunications systems.	1	2	3	4	9/
Domestic Commercial Airlines.	1	2	3	4	10/
Banking establishments.	1	2	3	4	11/
Large public gathering places (stadiums, malls, theater complexes, arenas).	1	2	3	4	12/
Public figures.	1	2	3	4	13/
Transportation systems.	1	2	3	4	14/
Utilities; energy, water.	1	2	3	4	15/

D7. During the next ten years, how likely do you think a major terrorist attack will occur in the United States? By major terrorist attack we mean one on a nuclear installation, or using chemical or biological weapons, or producing large number of casualties.

1. Very likely   16/
2. Somewhat likely
3. Not very likely
4. Not likely

D8. Has the likelihood of a major terrorist attack increased, decreased, or stayed the same during the last five years?

1. Increased   17/
2. Decreased
3. Stayed the same

D9. How likely do you think such an incident in your jurisdiction
is in the next ten years?

    1. Very likely   18/
    2. Somewhat likely
    3. Not very likely
    4. Not likely

D10. How well prepared are you to respond to such an incident?

    1. Very well prepared.   19/
    2. Well prepared.
    3. Somewhat prepared.
    4. Not well prepared.

SECTION E: ADMINISTRATIVE AND BUDGETARY INFORMATION

E1. What is the size of your department?

Sworn officers _____   20-22/

Support staff _____   23-25/

E2. Has your department added positions, lost positions, or stayed the same size in the last five years?

1. Added positions   26/
2. Lost positions
3. Remained the same

E3. What is your department's budget for the current fiscal year?

Payroll _____   27-33/

Facilities and equipment _____   34-40/

Total budget _____   41-50/

E4. Is this budget higher or lower than is was five years ago.

1. Higher   51/
2. Lower
3. Remained the same

E5. Does your department receive any federal funds?

1. Yes   52/
2. No

E6. What percentage of these funds are specifically allocated for counter- or anti-terrorism?

_____ %   53-54/

SECTION F: SUPPLEMENTAL INFORMATION

The following questions concern your assessment of your department's
abilities, needs and suggestions for addressing the threat of terrorism.

F10. What are your strengths? _____ 55-56/
_____ 57-58/
_____ 59-56/
_____
_____
_____
_____
_____
_____

F11. What are your weaknesses? _____ 57-58/
_____ 59-60/
_____ 61-62/
_____
_____
_____
_____
_____
_____

F12. What additional training do you require to increase your
level of preparedness?
_____ 63-64/
_____ 65-66/
_____ 67-68/
_____
_____
_____
_____
_____

|__|__|__| 1-3/
Card 06 4-5/

F13. What additional logistical resources do you need to increase
your level of preparedness?
_____ 6-7/
_____ 8-9/
_____ 10-11/
_____
_____
_____
_____
_____

F14. What additional intelligence do you require?

_____   12-13/
_____   14-15/
_____   16-17/
_____
_____
_____
_____
_____

F15. What additional open sources of information would be helpful
to you?

_____   18-19/
_____   20-21/
_____   22-23/
_____
_____
_____
_____
_____

F16. What specialized hardware is available to your agency for
anti- and counter-terrorist operations and procedures?

_____   24-25/
_____   26-27/
_____   28-29/
_____
_____
_____
_____

F17. What specialized hardware would be helpful to you?

_____   30-31/
_____   32-33/
_____   34-35/
_____
_____
_____
_____

****

Thank you for your participation. Please return this survey to:
RAND
ATTN: Jennifer Duncan
1700 Main Street
P.O. Box 2138
Santa Monica, CA 90406   (LCVer7/3)